THE MINDSET FITNESS WORKOUT

BE FIT FOR SUCCESS WITHOUT BURNING OUT

LUISA HOGAN

First published by Busybird Publishing 2025

Copyright © 2025 Luisa Hogan

ISBN:
Print: 978-1-923501-24-9

This work is copyright. Apart from any use permitted under the *Copyright Act 1968*, no part of this publication may be reproduced, stored in a retrieval system or transmitted in any form or by any means, electronic, mechanical, photocopying, recording or otherwise, without the prior written permission of Luisa Hogan

Cover Image: Luisa Hogan

Cover design: Luisa Hogan

Layout and typesetting: Busybird Publishing

Busybird Publishing
2/118 Para Road
Montmorency, Victoria
Australia 3094
www.busybird.com.au

Contents

About the Author	1
Foreword	5
Introduction	9

Part 1

The Mindset Fitness Program	19
1 - Marathons or Triathlons	21
2 - Creating a Fitness Plan	39
3 - Getting a Podium Finish	55
4 - Signing Up for the Next Race	65

Part 2

The Mindset Fitness Workouts	77
5 - Flexibility Training	79
Workouts for Flexibility	89
6 - Strength Training	99
Workouts for Strength	109
7 - Endurance Training	117
Workouts for Endurance and Resilience	127
8 - Composition Training	139
Workouts for Composition	147

Part 3

Mindset Fitness Benefits	155
9 - The Benefits of the Mindset Fitness Workouts	157
Conclusion	163

About the Author

Luisa Hogan has a passion for leadership, change, mindset and team resilience and is lucky enough to combine her passions through her work in her practice Vermelho. There, she works to help leaders improve their mindset so that they're ready for leading change. When she's not consulting on long-term projects, Luisa is an executive coach and international speaker. She's lived and worked in multiple countries, presented at conferences in Australia and overseas, and consulted on offshore projects in Cambodia.

Over the last decade, Luisa has led multiple business process reviews, restructures and change projects. She's been a state and national manager, chief operating officer, chief development officer and chief executive officer and volunteered on three not-for-profit boards. Luisa has been described as having an affinity for developing people and businesses to their highest potential, and was a state finalist in the Australian Institute of Management's Leadership Excellence Awards in 2017.

As a leader, she's witnessed how teams who increase their resilience and improve their mindset see better results, suffer less burnout and achieve their organisation's goals more effectively. These experiences have encouraged Luisa to build her knowledge and skills in these areas, which she's put to the test through challenging business transformations.

Luisa has a Bachelor of Arts in Education and Development Studies (Humanities), a Master of Business Administration (MBA), is a certified Change and Resilience Practitioner and has completed a

Specialised Certificate in Positive Psychology. In her spare time, Luisa has a passion for fitness and healthy living, having competed in multiple marathons, half-marathons and one triathlon. She's also a mindset coach for fellow runners looking to complete their first long distance race.

For Josh

My teamie through the biggest mental marathon I've faced so far, for cheering for me at finish lines, and for always providing fresh perspectives. He may well have the fittest mindset I've ever seen.

For my family

Always holding my hand, even from far away.

For my dad

Who taught me how to read, work hard, and generally 'keep it cool'. Forever loved and missed.

Foreword

Gemma Manning

I turned 40 recently and approached this milestone birthday by taking time to reflect on life's journey. After being in business for close to 12 years, two children later, divorce, then moving country to grow my two businesses internationally, my journey has been anything but ordinary. It's been a full life, a big life – lots of colour, lots of events, lots of excitement, but just as many challenges with plenty of curve balls thrown along the way.

I've experienced the roller-coaster ride of not only entrepreneurship, but life in general, and have had at times no option but to dig very deep and find the inner strength to travel my path and achieve my dreams and goals, all the while developing a strong mindset and emotional fitness.

So when my dear friend Luisa approached me to write this foreword for her book, I couldn't say no. Resilience and growth are two areas that I'm particularly passionate about, and to talk about this in the context of my own story is a great honour.

I met Luisa a few years ago at a CBA Women in Focus conference in Noosa, Queensland, Australia. I'd flown in from Singapore, my new base of operations at the time, to attend the all-female leader conference. I was the only Australian woman flying in from Asia for the event. I didn't know anyone, and I felt strange coming back into

Australia, leaving my two daughters in Singapore for the third trip back to Australia that month. I hoped that it would be worth the effort.

Luisa was the first person that I met, and immediately we connected – some might say it was a cosmic connection. When I learnt that Luisa specialised in resilience and mindset, I was fascinated, and hungry to learn more. You see, I had not been taught about resilience and had to learn the hard way about how to have a healthy mindset and how to bounce back to survive – whether in my personal or business life.

I've often wondered why I am the way I am. I'm a high-achiever – always have been – and I'm someone who likes to set goals *and* achieve the goals that I set. This stems from when I was at 10 years of age. I was in Year 5 at primary school in Cairns. I remember my teacher commenting that a girl had never won the annual excellence award before. So I set myself the challenge to win; after all, why shouldn't' girls win? To my delight, I won the award that year. I worked hard, was focused and never wavered – I was determined! I still have the Henry Lawson book of poetry that I won on my bookshelf at home all these years later – it's symbolic for me.

From that point on, I've never been any different always setting goals – whether it be personal or business, I've always set goals, had a road map to achieve those goals, and been focused on the job at hand.

This hasn't always been easy or gone to plan. There have been many hurdles and obstacles. I've asked myself: why do I have to be a high achiever constantly pushing the boundaries? It's taken me 40 years to accept who I am.

But when I met Luisa, I still had so many questions about my very nature. I'd never taken a course before in resilience. I've learnt the hard way, and I only wish I had some earlier exposure to mindset and resilience skills development, and met Luisa 20 years ago! Thank goodness she's in my life now. She's helped me to understand the mindset you need to have when you're the kind of person forever setting goals and why resilience is so important. For this, I will forever be grateful.

It's been a 5 year journey to build a solid business in Asia. It's taken significant time, resources, investment and sacrifice. Not to mention hard work, risk and a great deal of courage and bravery too. I can only now say that I've achieved what I set out to achieve – a sustainable business that services companies across the APAC region with solid business growth from my Singapore headquarters.

Only a year ago, I was ready to throw it all in. I've had so many challenges that I could dedicate a book to this alone. From being greeted with hostility from several parties protective of their Singapore patch, to government departments poaching my clients, to IP being stolen, to wrong hiring decisions that cost significantly – growing a business from Australia into Asia hasn't gone the way I expected. There's been more travel than I thought, more time away from my girls having to leave them in another country without the usual support network… the list goes on.

To overcome these challenges, I've had to show resilience, agility, open-mindedness and willingness to be flexible and go where the opportunities are.

It's been one of the hardest times in my life and the most difficult mountain I've had to climb. It's tested me every other day, and I've often questioned my decision to grow into Asia. I've moved my girls away from their dad in Sydney. I'm away from my family who I'm so close to and adore. I've lost some of my core business in Australia because of the move. The stakes have been high.

I've been close to burning out – it's taken every ounce of energy from me to get here. This experience, especially the last 3 years, has been all-consuming. I've often been in survival mode. I've often lost motivation and wanted to throw in the towel and go home.

However, I managed to remain focused, picked myself up and kept going when I thought it was humanly impossible. My support network and loving family, especially my daughters, have been both inspiration and motivation that truly kept me going. Their support and unconditional love is everything. I'm a role model to my girls as well as to many other young women and I'm motivated to make a positive change and difference when it comes to gender equality through this journey.

Looking back on the last 3 years since moving to Singapore, without a doubt there are many things that I would do differently – but hindsight is a wonderful thing. I know that I need to manage my stress levels and take more time out to reflect, reset and refocus. I also need to introduce more meditation into my routine and practise more gratitude rather than being so hard on myself.

I'm comfortable in being proud of what I've achieved and not apologising for it as I have in the past. I'm also happy to have finally accepted who I am. It's okay for me to want to constantly challenge myself, extend myself, grow and live a bigger life through my dreaming and goal-setting. And I've learnt too that the biggest dreamers and achievers are also life-long learners and are not afraid to ask for advice or learn from others.

So I can't wait to learn more through this book. Thank you, Luisa, for bringing your insights, tips and learnings to us all. Whether it's in our personal or business life, we can all learn how to follow our dreams, achieve our goals and implement our ideas.

Gemma Manning

Founder & Group CEO – Manning and Co

Managing Director – Gemstar

Introduction

In 2015, I found myself excited to start a new role as chief operating officer in a small consultancy after being head-hunted by the new chief executive officer there. On my first day of work, my heart sank when I discovered my first task was to make 70% of the roles in the organisation redundant.

This business had experienced several changes with their contractor's needs but had not been entirely successful in implementing changes fast enough to adapt to the changing needs of their market. They were on the path to losing a significant source of funding and their new CEO of 6 months had to make some drastic decisions.

The remaining team felt demoralised and uncertain about their future. Their most significant client of 20 years was signalling that they were going to withdraw their contract in just 2 years. Since 90% of the organisation's income rested with this one contract, we had some work to do! Not only was I required to rebuild trust with the team, but we had to find a way to bring in new contracts into the business. As a team, we had to set a new vision, create new goals, and try to find solutions. Unfortunately, this was just the start of our challenges. Less than a year after I started in the role, our CEO resigned, and I stepped into the role, with the mandate of keeping the organisation alive.

At this point, our primary contractor shortened their contract period to just 12 months and changed the terms of payment. The added time and finance pressure created a threat of further redundancy. I needed to find a way to inspire the team and set them working towards a meaningful goal that they all related to, and that allowed us to grow the business. To do this, I had to cultivate psychological safety within the team, and together we created a new vision, found new sales pipelines and transformed our reputation so that our business was more secure.

Our funding mix was now at 60% with the primary contractor instead of 90%. We began to grow more confident as we now felt we had time on our side to make a more significant shift. We felt more connected and trusting as a team. Morale improved, and so did consultant performance. It seemed we had turned a corner, with more purpose and a more sustainable future that did not rely on a single major contract.

Sadly, on a single day, this came apart.

We lost our major contract 12 months sooner than we'd initially anticipated. Before this, I'd been working with our Board of Directors to build a new strategy. But now they had to decide on whether to continue the path of our new vision or avoid risk and close the business. With a new pipeline of work not fully over the line and with the direction of the organisation having changed entirely, the Board decided to close the organisation. I had to tell my entire hard-working team that they would be helping me to wind up what they'd created.

What happened next was extraordinary. I still regard this as one of the most profound experiences of my life. My team had built a healthy level of trust and meaning over the previous months, which allowed them to support each other to wrap up our old and new contracts professionally and wind up our business with our heads held high. They looked after all of the new clients that we'd worked hard to attain. I'm immensely proud of the mindset the team had to make that happen. I could not abandon them because they did not abandon me, and I will be forever grateful for the lessons they taught me. We had just run a mental marathon together, and we made it to the end in one piece, albeit a bit bruised.

That experience was the start of my practice – Vermelho – in 2017. Vermelho was born from my desire to prevent other leaders from experiencing the devastating effects of poorly managing change.

And also from my passion for building resilient teams, just like the one I'd left.

Through the resulting countless consulting projects I've led, through coaching many executives, and through all the discussions I have had speaking at conferences and delivering workshops, I've often asked myself 'Why is it that people don't improve their mindset fitness? Why do we know to train for marathons, but we don't know how to train for mental marathons?' And so, I started to develop a Mindset Fitness model that propels people and teams towards achieving their goals.

So, what do I mean by 'mental marathons'? Naturally, it's what happens when we have complex goals that take a long time to achieve. My experience as the CEO of that consultancy is an example of this. Other examples are visionary strategic goals, lofty KPIs, optimistic income targets, and broad transformation project goals. Personally, it could be finishing an MBA, undertaking a career change, or starting a business. We continuously generate change. The mental demands on goal pursuits such as these are akin to running a mental marathon and demands resilience and growth mindsets.

Through my work, I began to imagine a world where we paid attention to our mindset fitness as much as we do to our physical fitness. In the same way that neglecting our nutrition and physical exercise can cause health problems, neglecting mindset fitness can cause problems with achieving goals, staying the course, and maintaining resilience when goals seem overwhelming. We lose willpower. We lose the ability to see the way forward. Mindset workouts are as important as muscle workouts.

When a challenging event or circumstance arises, we must have the mindset fitness to respond positively or risk a decline in the mental will to continue the pursuit of the goal and potentially even a drop in psychological wellbeing. And with the rapid change that occurs around us, we need people with the right mindset to face those challenges.

This book is my response to my experiences, and the findings of so many great authors and researchers. You will find that many of the concepts in this book are not new. You will find them in individual books of their own, written by many talented authors, psychologists and researchers. I reference many of them should you like to explore a concept in more detail.

What I've done is bring all these ideas together to create a Mindset Fitness model that helps you exercise your mindset so that it becomes a habit. The model is not only based on good emotional intelligence, positive psychology and mindset research. It also brings together the work I've done with my clients on mindset and change, and through what I apply in my goal-setting. It's helped me to grow a successful practice and train for multiple marathons (the running kind). It's helped me read a book a week for over 12 months. And it's allowed me to coach multiple people to achieve their goals. I know that with these Mindset Fitness Workouts, you too will be able to take part in the mental marathons we all regularly face today.

The importance of goals

All of us have experience with goal-setting. Some only with the ubiquitous 'New Year's resolution' but many of us use goal-setting processes effectively throughout the year, to try to focus efforts and increase personal performance. Others experience goal-setting at work, with businesses using strategic goals and KPIs to propel their mission or profits forward.

Even so, the reality is that many feel frustrated around setting goals, vaguely feeling like they should be setting them but not knowing how to make them work for them. A whopping 88% of New Year's resolutions fail, according to a 2007 survey of over 3000 people conducted by British psychologist Richard Wiseman.

Many people set random goals based on extrinsic motivators. In a work environment, chances are that many allow their manager or supervisor to set goals for them. This can be wasteful if they don't connect with the intent of the target or see it as meaningful for them. I mainly know this type of goal-setting to occur in change projects, where senior leaders set goals for change, and the goals have no meaningful connection to their teams. Or at least, the links aren't communicated in a way that means something to their organisations.

Studies as far back as the early 90s showed the role of organisational goal-setting as critical to the continued long-term success of that organisation. The *Management Research News* stated that realistically developed, stated, and implemented goals can be the guiding principle for increased effectiveness and continued growth, while the lack of effective goal-setting leads to decline in an organisation's performance (Cochran & Kleiner, 1992).

To many, goal-setting seems like a relatively simple process. You think about what you want to achieve, you write it down, and then you make it happen. The reality is that goal-setting is rather complicated and confusing. Do you choose to run a marathon? Or do you decide to try out a triathlon? Do you grow the business, or do you consolidate?

Using goal-setting effectively can be a surprise challenge and can be further exacerbated by fixed mindsets that prevent people from seeing opportunities in failures. And it's not enough to record a goal and write it down either. Thinking is not the same as doing.

In her book, *The How of Happiness: A Scientific Approach to Getting the Life You Want*, psychology researcher Sonja Lyubomirsky points out six specific benefits goal-setting can bring to wellbeing. She uses the term 'committed goal pursuit' to emphasise that we're not just talking about creating lists of goals, but that we're focused on the process of following through with them. Lyubomirsky's list states that meaningful goals, as follows:

1. Give a sense of purpose and a feeling of control to our lives

Everyone has experienced a time in their lives where they weren't pursuing a specific goal. For short periods, it might be nice to have a break from these guides on how to focus our time and attention. But over the long term, it can be draining and demotivating. Many people find retirement quite a letdown when they suddenly find themselves free of the responsibilities that had shaped their lives for decades. Similar results can occur when an employee's role has been made redundant, and they find themselves unemployed. Our brains and our bodies are designed to be actively working to shape our lives. We feel at home having goals, and feel lost without them. I feel at my best when I'm working towards a running goal or on a contract with a client.

2. Increase self-esteem and can also motivate us to continue to exert effort towards further goals

When we work towards something meaningful, and we see results, it can give us a boost of joy and pride. These positive emotions are enjoyable, and they also can motivate us to continue to exert effort towards further goals. By not having goals we're working toward, we can feel disconnected or may have a sense of boredom and apathy. Even though it's not always easy or fun to work towards a goal, it does bring us a sense of satisfaction.

3. Add structure and interest to our daily lives

We can't get to where we want to go without doing different things, and without learning new things that help us master new skills and broaden our perspectives. As we move through our days, we focus on the tasks that must be accomplished to get us to our desired ends. These tasks involve variety, and they frequently include growth.

4. Help us learn to strategise and prioritise our time

Complex goals must be broken down into smaller steps and, in turn, we must prioritise the order in which we wish to pursue them.

5. Can be helpful to us in times of crisis

Provided we're still able to accomplish the goals, they can help keep us grounded in times of change or uncertainty. For example, during a significant business disruption, giving employees clear tasks and goals to accomplish can be a welcome activity that helps them move forward rather than panic.

6. Frequently bring us into contact with other people

In the pursuit of goals, we have to work with others through collaboration, helping us feel more deeply connected in our relationships and communities.

Why people don't follow through with their goals

It's clear then that goals are important! So why is it that many fail at practical goal-setting? Why do so few people follow through on their goals?

Back in 1994, C R Snyder published a book called *The Psychology of Hope*. In that book, he defines hope as 'the sum of the mental willpower and way power that you have for your goals'. The definition has three key terms: goals, willpower, and 'way power'. Goals are the destination on a journey. Willpower is motivation, and is the fuel you'll use to achieve the goals. And the way power is the map or GPS that you'll use to figure out how to get there.

To move towards our goals effectively, we need to have a clear sense of what our goals are. We also need plenty of motivation to move towards them and enough alternate routes that we can continue to move forward, even when one pathway is blocked.

Some people have plenty of willpower and way power, but are hindered with unclear or non-meaningful goals. They have plenty of fuel, and a large fuel tank for their car, a great map and GPS, but a lack of destination.

Others have different concerns. Maybe they have a clear goal, and creative ideas for how to get there, but they can't seem to get started. They lack motivation or fuel!

Or maybe they have a clear goal, and plenty of motivation, but have no idea what the first few steps should be. Or perhaps their pathway became blocked and they couldn't figure out how to move around the obstacle.

Snyder emphasises the importance of controlling attention robbers, having the mindset to see challenges as motivators and suggests we break up long-term goals into smaller steps. He also suggests practising laying out different routes to your goals and then selecting the best one. Not only does this keep you focused on your goals, but it can help you find more efficient and productive pathways to achieving them. Also, it can prepare us with alternate routes if our preferred path is no longer an option.

Snyder's final suggestion is that we must be willing and able to ask for help. There are always others who have walked the same path as you before. Or who may have advice for you on how to achieve a goal.

There's also some great work by Gabriele Oettingen, a professor of psychology at New York University and the University of Hamburg in Germany. In her book, *Rethinking Positive Thinking*, Oettingen begins by pointing out that we should avoid imagining that we have already attained our goals. Even though we are often told to visualise success, her research indicates that those who imagine that they have already accomplished their goal are less motivated to take the actions necessary to get it. Consequently, they are less likely to make it a reality.

So what does work?

Oettingen identifies two approaches. Namely, mental contrasting and implementation intentions. Despite their rather academic-sounding names, these processes are relatively simple. Mental contrasting begins with fantasising about reaching the goal, but with an extra step. The key is to imagine that you have reached a challenging but obtainable goal then immediately contrast that with obstacles that stand in the way of you realising that goal. Examples could be negative thoughts or attitudes, or behaviours and habits.

The exercise can be a powerful motivator to help you overcome the roadblocks you imagined and increase the likelihood that you will reach your goal. The second practical approach for following through on our goals that Oettingen identifies in her book is implementation intentions, or an 'if–then' plan for how to tackle an obstacle to your goal. For example, if you're training for a marathon, what will you do if you get a minor injury? Knowing your plan for an obstacle makes it more likely that you will stick to your goal.

This book and your goals

By reading on, you will learn to commit to meaningful goals, and work to improve your mindset fitness to achieve those goals. Part 1 of the book sets out the steps you will need to take in the Mindset Fitness model. Part 2 describes each fitness area and the workouts you can choose to help you in those areas. And Part 3 lays out the benefits you will see as you progress.

The workouts are not designed to be another big task to add to your already busy day. The idea is to commit to small workouts often rather than long sessions occasionally. Each workout is designed to take only a few minutes out of your day, and each is prescribed for different mindsets you would like to achieve. You can pick and choose the best workouts for you at any given time to assist you with an obstacle you're facing. You may choose to focus on one particular area for a while. Or, you may decide to have a mix of workouts from all focus areas. It is up to you!

Bibliography

Cochran, T. & Kleiner, B. H. (1992). Effective Organisational Goal Setting. *Management Research News*, 15(9), pp. 13–17. Retrieved from https://emerald.com/insight/content/doi/10.1108/eb028260/full/html.

Karp, T. (2014). Leaders need to develop their willpower. *Journal of Management Development*, 33(3), pp. 150–163. Retrieved from https://emerald.com/insight/content/doi/10.1108/jmd-04-2012-0051/full/html.

Lyubomirsky, S. (2008). *The How of Happiness*. New York: Penguin Books.

Oettingen, G. (2015). *Rethinking Positive Thinking: Inside the New Science of Motivation*. New York: Random House.

Snyder, C. (1994). *The Psychology of Hope*. New York: Free Press.

Wiseman, R. (2019). Quirkology – Experiment – Resolution Experiment. Retrieved November 11, 2019, from http://www.richardwiseman.com/quirkology/new/USA/Experiment_resolution.shtml.

Part 1

The Mindset Fitness Program

The following four chapters provide you with details on the four steps you will take on the Mindset Fitness Program, as shown in the following diagram.

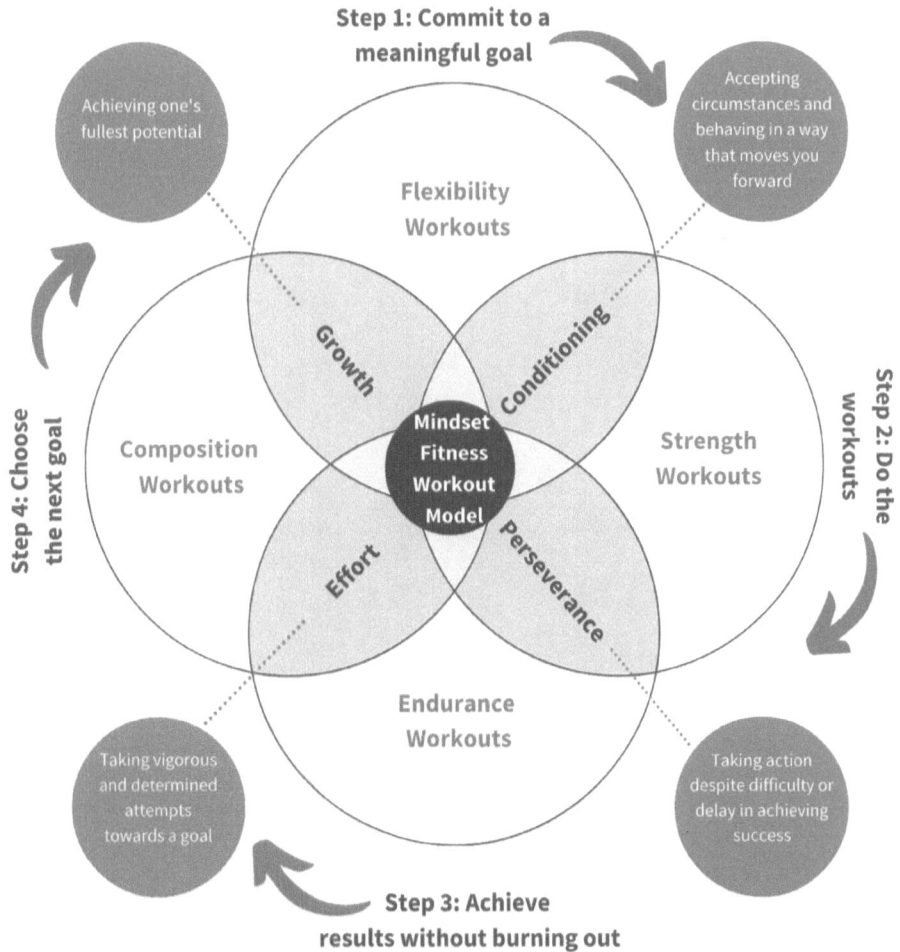

1

Marathons or Triathlons

'Desire is the key to motivation, but it's determination and commitment to an unrelenting pursuit of your goal – a commitment to excellence – that will enable you to attain the success you seek.'

Mario Andretti

Step 1: Committing to meaningful goals

In 2012, Janine Chatfield became a mum. She was fit and healthy and had a dream pregnancy until her daughter was born 9 weeks early at 31 weeks gestation. The event was traumatic for her, being a first-time mother and having to leave her premature baby in the neonatal intensive care unit for 6 weeks.

It was both mentally and physically challenging, and it had a significant impact on Janine. Months after her daughter's birth, and once they'd settled back at home, Janine decided to see what was out there to help parents such as her deal with the challenges of premature babies.

Janine found an organisation called the Miracle Babies Foundation, the aim of which is to support families that have sick or newborn premature babies. At the time, they were advertising for runners to join the Miracle Babies Foundation New York Marathon team, to raise money and awareness for the foundation. Janine had been a runner for several years, having completed countless fun runs and half marathons, but the idea of a full marathon just felt completely out of her reach. But, now that she had become a mother, she saw herself as a 'lioness'.

So, Janine set the goal to join the team for her daughter and for parents that have or will have a similar experience. Janine wanted to show her daughter that mothers are strong and fierce and determined and that they're not just mums but women with individual goals and dreams that can be achieved even under challenging circumstances.

Janine faced many obstacles during her training. Throughout this time, Janine's husband, Ryan, was a FIFO worker and would spend 4 weeks away at work. While Ryan was away at work, Janine's training consisted of doing short runs with the pram, and during nap times she would run on the treadmill.

Janine lost toenails, had significant ITB pain (a tendon on the side of the leg), experienced self-doubt and had an insatiable craving to eat pasta for 6 months. She also had to raise a minimum of $10,000 to be eligible to join the team to run the New York Marathon. Additionally, she had to pay for the expense of flying to the USA.

Even so, at the forefront of her mind was her daughter and the example she was setting for her. Also, the number of friends, families and strangers that donated money, goods and services to her fundraising efforts certainly kept her motivated and accountable. She spent the days with her daughter, and although she loved every single moment with her, she also needed to do something that was just for her – running allowed her to take time out for herself.

Janine was able to achieve her goal because of the considerable support network she had in place. She raised over $10,000 for the Miracle Babies Foundation and ran 42.2 km through five boroughs of New York City.

It didn't all go according to plan. Janine was severely injured going into the race. When she arrived in NYC 10 days before the marathon, she couldn't walk let alone run. Her ITB had flared, and there was a knot in her hip flexor the size and consistency of a golf ball. After countless dry needling sessions and physiotherapy in Australia, and a tedious search for a sports masseuse in NYC, she was able to work the knot down to the size of a grape. She hadn't stepped out for a run for 3 weeks before the race because she couldn't do it! She was plagued with doubt the day before the marathon and was terrified she would let everyone down. But it was a conversation with the masseuse that put things into perspective for her. She moved her goalposts. Initially, she wanted to run the marathon in a time of under 4 hours. But the masseuse said that the cut-off time for the marathon was 8 hours. If Janine tried only to complete it, then she had time on her side. She could walk it if she had to. That shift in perspective took the pressure off.

When Janine lined up at the start line, she was full of anxiety. The event had almost been cancelled due to an extreme weather warning that morning and potentially dangerous conditions. It was cold, wet, and windy. And she was injured. When the gun went off, and Janine pushed off for her first run in weeks, something indescribable happened. The pain left her, and euphoria arrived. She ran a consistent pace, but also stopped to take photos and dance with some of the one million spectators that had come out to cheer on the runners. She didn't make her initial goal time, but she ran the entire way and crossed the finish line in Central Park. She also made the time cut-off to have her name listed in the *New York Times*.

When I asked Janine what lessons she learned, she told me this:

'The New York Marathon taught me so many things; it highlighted that with the right mindset, grit, hard work and support network, you could chase down your dreams. Because of this experience, I don't put limitations on myself. I know if I want it badly enough, I'll make it happen. Fundraising for Miracle Babies taught me about resilience, how to be flexible and to keep going. Chipping away at a goal may take a week, a year or 10 years. But don't sit idly, it won't come to you. Back yourself. You've got this.'

What is a meaningful goal?

How does one identify truly meaningful goals? The word 'meaningful' is used to describe something that has a purpose. You would probably say that undertaking a degree is meaningful or worthwhile, but you might not describe 3 hours watching bad TV shows as meaningful. When something is important or significant, it is meaningful, or 'full of meaning'. Looking at Janine's goal, you can see that it was not insignificant to her. It had a purpose, and it linked to experiences that had no small impact on her.

The search for purpose and meaning in life has become more and more important for people in this century. Dr Viktor Emil Frankl (1905–1997), a Viennese psychiatrist and neurologist, is most famous for his best-selling novel *Man's Search for Meaning*. His book outlines his horrific experiences in the concentration camps of World War II. Frankl was subjected to four different Nazi camps and was dehumanised to a mere number. Moreover, Nazis murdered his wife, mother, father, and unborn child, yet Frankl was able to find a purpose for living in all his sufferings (Frankl, 1959).

Many of us become so wrapped up in the day-to-day demands of daily life that we end up forgetting, deferring or neglecting our more meaningful passions. Our abandoned desires impact our long-term happiness, and research suggests this can turn into regrets that refuse to go away.

So how do we distinguish between meaningful goals and goals that are less so? Let's look again at a few tips taken from Sonja Lyubomirsky's *The How of Happiness* and also work from Heidi Halvorson. They explain different types of goals and how some can be more meaningful than others.

Intrinsic and extrinsic goals

We pursue intrinsic goals because we find them inherently valuable and satisfying. They connect us with our interests and help us grow as people and they even help us connect with others. They nurture our most basic need for autonomy. They make us feel like we're in control of ourselves, they give us feelings of competence and like we have mastery over our environment, and give us feelings of relatedness as though we are connected to others.

Janine's goal had an intrinsic nature. It allowed her to pursue something that was part of her running identity and allowed her to connect with others for support. A study by the Economic Science Institute in 2012 showed that an intrinsically motivated person felt more rewarded and satisfied by achieving their goal than those with no intrinsic motivation. They tested this by paying some participants for completing a specific goal, and then not paying others but asking them to set goals to their standards (Gómez-Miñambres, 2012).

On the other hand, extrinsic goals are valued instrumentally for something else they can provide us, and they often connect to what other people think of us. Goals for being wealthy, being beautiful, having a fancy work title and being famous are examples of extrinsic goals. If we want to maximise our ability to achieve our goals, we should remember that things like financial success and power are extrinsic goals. They are valuable not in themselves, but for what they can bring. If you are a leader, you should also consider whether your team has intrinsic or extrinsic goals.

Flexible and appropriate goals

Flexible and appropriate goals consider the stage of life we're in, the abilities we have, and the norms of the culture around us. Lyubomirsky (2008) states that younger people tend to prioritise expanding their knowledge and establishing their future. Examples of goals for them include things like getting an education, embarking on a career, buying a house, getting married, or having children. On the flip side of the coin, older people tend to focus more on emotionally meaningful goals, since they usually have already achieved the goals from their youth – Janine's goal linked to a new stage in her life – that of becoming a mother.

Besides the differences in the stages of life we are in, there may also be unexpected changes in our health, finances, or family situations that we take into consideration when setting goals. Remaining inflexible in such cases can work against us. Being realistic and creative in those situations can support our motivation to stay the course. I often say that we hold onto old fears, dreams and hopes in our minds like we sometimes hold onto old clothes that no longer fit us. Those old fears and hopes no longer suit us yet unduly influence us. By cleaning out the 'wardrobes' in our minds and letting go of those old fears and dreams, we can be more flexible and appropriate with our goal-setting.

Activity and circumstances goals

Lyubomirsky (2008) suggests that choosing goals that involve taking up a new activity are better than goals for improving our circumstances. There is research that indicates that we are likely to adapt quickly to the enhanced wellbeing brought by better material items like a new TV or car. We may feel happier in the short term, but the novelty soon wears off, and the latest thing becomes the new normal. Take a look at Janine's goal. It clearly illustrates how she took up a new challenge of fundraising and running the marathon. Things could have been different if her goals were more about changing her material circumstances.

Activity goals are more resistant to adaptation because they open us up to novelty on an ongoing basis. For example, learning a new skill in a workshop or through a university course opens us up to a range of new experiences. They prepare us for even more novel experiences as we continue to apply what we have learnt in new ways. Joining a running club, for example, allows us to share new experiences. This lasts much longer than the joy of owning a new car.

Why and what goals

Heidi Grant Halvorson makes some useful distinctions in her book *Succeed: How We Can Reach Our Goals*. She describes 'why' versus 'what' goals.

Imagine it's Monday morning, and you need to spend some time sorting out your filing and administration that has been piling up over previous weeks. What would be the goal you set yourself to rectify this? You could write down 'tidy up admin papers' as an example of a 'why' goal. Labelling it in this way explains the purpose of the actions you were planning to undertake (for example, to tidy up your admin). You know 'why' you have to do it.

Alternatively, you could write down 'sort through admin, shred duplicates and file notes' as an example of a 'what' goal. Writing it this way explains the actions you intend to take, which are shredding and sorting and filing.

Although each goal involves similar activities, different situations call for you to think of your efforts in terms of 'why' goals, and other times in terms of 'what' goals. Halvorson's book points out that 'why' goals help us get energised, stay motivated, and avoid temptation. Alternatively, 'what' goals are particularly helpful with challenging tasks, unfamiliar tasks, and tasks that take a long time to learn because they give you the steps you need to take.

Be good and get better goals

Halvorson (2014) points out that 'be good' versus 'get better' goals are the difference between proving yourself and improving yourself. You would use each in a different situation. When you have a simple situation, and you want to focus on performing well, then using 'be good' goals is an excellent course of action. For example, if you're an amateur long-distance runner, running a 5 km race may be easy for you. A 'be good' goal would be to come in one of the top ten places in the race.

In more complex situations, Halvorson recommends using 'get better' goals. These types of goals are focused on improving performance and help you to enjoy the journey and not just the destination. They also fight depression and help you to achieve more. Using the amateur runner example again, if you plan on running your first marathon, you're probably better off setting a goal like finishing the marathon in a particular time and improving the time in a second marathon. If your goal is a 'be good' goal to win the marathon, doing poorly on your first attempt can be demoralising, and you may feel like your goal is unattainable. But adopting the goal of getting a better time on your second race, you have something real to shoot for, and are more likely to result in improved performance. Janine's goals for her marathon time perfectly illustrate this.

Prevention and promotion goals

Sonja Lyubomirsky differentiates between 'prevention' and 'promotion' types of goals. An example of prevention goals will be if you are preparing to do your driver's licence exam for the first time. Your goal would likely be to not to fail the test. Prevention goals like this keep us calm when we succeed. They also make us less likely to try new things. They do help us plan better, avoid procrastination, and focus on details. Prevention goals are most useful when we need accuracy over speed as they help us avoid distractions and temptations. We become more focused on not failing, and therefore it's challenging to think of anything else.

In contrast, promotion goals aid you with optimism. Let's say your goal is to be a keynote presenter at a conference and to have a successful presentation. That's a promotion goal, and it means that we will be happy when we succeed and sad when we fail. Promotion goals lead to greater creativity and exploratory thinking. And they're especially useful when we need speed over accuracy. Halverson argues each of these two types of goals has a time and place and that different people benefit more from one or the other.

Lyubomirsky also points out that people who make a habit of pursuing promotion goals tend to have higher wellbeing than those who seek prevention goals. While both are important, it's probably best to go with promotion goals whenever you can.

How to set meaningful goals

The first step in the Mindset Fitness Program is to set a meaningful goal. But as you can see, it can be challenging to know what direction to take. So how should you go about choosing meaningful goals? We live in a world where we have so much more choice and freedom, and this can be paralysing.

On the one hand, we know that having clear and meaningful goals means that on the days we're less motivated, we still feel committed to the goal. On the other hand, it's easier said than done to find our passions and meaningful goals.

When I was in school, I thought that if only I knew what my life purpose was, I would be happy to pursue it. Unfortunately, I liked many different school subjects and was able to excel at a few of them. I envied classmates who were outstanding in one subject because it was visible to them what pathway they should choose.

One particular classmate was a gun at mathematics and declared in Year 10 that she was going to become an actuary. I believe she went on to do this. She found her direction in life early on. I thought that perhaps one day, I would have an epiphany of sorts. After school, I enrolled in a triple-major degree with three completely different areas of expertise. And later in my career, I went on to complete an MBA. I think I've since found passions in entirely unrelated subjects. My passions evolved and the direction of my life has emerged from there.

It would have been fantastic to have some instructions over the years on how to set meaningful goals that pinpointed what was important to me.

So here are a variety of methods for you to find goals that are meaningful to you.

Method 1: Your wishes for the future

Earlier on, I mentioned the research by Oettingen. She came up with something that was even more effective in helping people reach their goals. She developed what she calls WOOP. WOOP is an easy-to-learn mental strategy that brings you closer to your desires and turns dreams into achievable goals (WOOP my life, 2019).

WOOP stands for:

Wish

With this method, you begin by identifying what you would wish for the future. Take time to imagine yourself 30 years from now. What would you qualify as missed opportunities? What would you regret not pursuing? These are likely the things that are most meaningful to you.

Outcome

Now connect to the outcome by imagining you have already achieved your wish. What will happen as a consequence? How do you feel?

Obstacle

Identify an internal obstacle that's holding you back from reaching this goal. You imagine that obstacle as clearly and powerfully as you can.

Plan

Create an if/then plan for what you will do when you encounter that obstacle. You may need to adjust and practise this a few times to make it work well for you.

Method 2: Reflective practice

In the book, *Grit: The Power of Passion of Perseverance* by Angela Duckworth, she gives what I think is excellent advice to those like me who never got the lightning bolt telling us what to do with our lives. She describes how lightning bolt moments are more fairytale than reality. Although some people can pinpoint early experiences that put them on their life path, in virtually all those cases, those first experiences could have also led them down many different ways.

People often have several experiences that could lead them in very different directions. Older people need to have a strong narrative to support their life choices. But those narratives typically come after the decisions have been made, and not before. Indeed, I found this happened with my own experiences.

Having grown up in Africa, I had been exposed to nature and animals and safaris all my life. My much older brother and sister went on to pursue careers in zoology and nature conservation. So by the time I had to choose a career, I decided on what I already knew.

After a year in university studying zoology, I decided that I was more interested in education, geography, community development and English! I changed my degree and graduated, intending to teach high-school geography and English. When I immigrated to Australia in my early 20s, I found myself working temporarily for a not-for-profit organisation working with children. It was the right temporary place for my education skills.

I was promoted to team leader and later, manager, and I found myself having a passion for leadership. My path took many twists and turns, with my experience making me an expert in managing change and leading teams. I completed my MBA and found myself as a CEO for a consultancy working with aged care, disability and mental health organisations. This eventually led me to start my practice as a change and resilience consultant and mindset coach. The narrative for supporting my life choices came after I had made many choices. I gained clarity on my passions as I journeyed through my options. Chances are it has taken most of us a long time to get to a point of clarity in our lives. My story, no doubt, could have taken a lot of different directions.

So how do you develop your goals if you don't yet have them clearly in mind? I think Duckworth's advice is excellent. She says it's essential not just to follow your passion, but to foster it. Like Duckworth, I don't believe passion is just something you're born with or that usually emerges naturally throughout your childhood. For most people, it's something they have to foster. Duckworth says cultivating interests is a better way to go. Her book describes three specific steps for doing that.

Discover

Duckworth recommends asking yourself questions such as: What do I like to think about? Where does my mind wander? What do I care about? What matters most to me? How do I enjoy spending my time?

And, in contrast, you should ask questions such as: What do I find unbearable? Duckworth suggests that if you're unsure about what your natural interests are, think back to what you might have said as a teenager since this is when interests often start to emerge. Think about what you enjoy doing. What makes the time fly by? What do you wish you could do more of? That's where the magic of goal-setting happens. If you set a goal around what you're excited about, you are more likely to achieve it.

Experiment

Once you have a few answers written down, it's time to experiment. Try doing some of the activities you chose and see if your interest in them increases, decreases or remains the same.

Develop

Once you've discovered or experimented with your interests, spend time engaging with them and getting a deeper appreciation for why you connect with them. Spend time with others who share your interests. Or perhaps find a mentor who can give you good advice and who will help deepen your knowledge and expertise and who'll help your interest grow and mature.

Deepen

It's common for us to lose some of our initial interest in something once we are adept at it and we may have an urge to try something new. Instead, focus on ways to enjoy the nuances of an activity that only a master can appreciate. In that way, you may foster your passion to the point that it provides you with life goals.

Method 3: Get clear on your vision, values, and priorities

Your values, vision and priorities are like a life compass. They give you direction and keep you on track if you stay aware of them. A life compass tool is available below, but for now, it's crucial to understand why your values, vision and priorities influence goal-setting.

Vision

A vision is about seeing the bigger picture. Your life's vision defines what you want to be known for, and what accomplishments you want to achieve, and who you want to be. Your vision helps you identify goals by giving a robust framework to evaluate your goals. Your vision becomes the reason why you're pursuing those goals.

Your vision should aim to answer questions like:

- *What do I want to have done with my life by the time I've lived to age 20, 30, 40, 50, 60, 70 and 80?*

- *What kinds of people do I want to be surrounded by?*

- *What do I believe I'm capable of in life? What are the most important things I could accomplish, given the right circumstances, resources and motivation?*

- *What do I wish I could change about the world? What could I contribute to the world that would make me feel proud and content?*

Your goals should align with this vision. Goals that don't bring you closer to your vision are probably not worth setting.

Values

Being clear about your values gives you the best chance of achieving your goals. Goals are typically challenging and usually geared towards the future. Values keep you motivated, and without them, you might not persist when you bump into challenges (Eccles and Wigfield, 2002).

When you pursue a goal that's out of alignment with your core values, it can potentially lead to failure and disappointment. By using your values to set personal and meaningful goals, you will feel excited and unstoppable. Each step you take towards achieving your goal, you will know you're standing for something and doing something meaningful with your life. Imagine the satisfaction and fulfilment when this occurs.

A simple way to find your values is to ask yourself 'How do I want to be remembered when I'm gone?' It sounds morbid, but I doubt anyone would say, 'I want to be remembered for being rich.' They're more likely to say 'I want to be remembered for being hard-working, wise, kind and generous.'

To create a list of things you want to be remembered for, think of personality traits you admire, values you believe firmly in, and the experiences you enjoy.

Priorities

A life compass tool can be seen below. Each box has a different area in your life that you either prioritise or not prioritise.

Personal growth	Leisure	Spirituality
Health	Work	Community
Family	Partner	Social

In the top square of each box, rank from 1 to 10 how important this area of your life is to you. You can rank different areas the same.

In the bottom square of each box, rate from 1 to 10 how well you feel you're focusing on this area of your life.

Now make notes about what you want to improve in each area so that you increase focus on the critical areas in your life.

Finally, you can ask if the goals you've set contribute to how you want to be remembered and to your vision and values.

A word on commitment

Sometimes people fail in goals because they're trying to practise discipline before they become committed. To achieve meaningful goals, you must become mentally dedicated to creating what you desire, despite what you face. Commitment starts in the mind and manifests when practised in your discipline. You will know you're committed and have discipline when nobody tells you what you must do to achieve your goal.

When you've decided on a meaningful goal and commit to it, it becomes something that you *must* achieve. Because you must meet your goals, you can't merely set then forget them. You will find yourself needing to work or implement actions that will lead to that achievement.

If you don't have an obligation to achieve your goals, how can you expect to maintain the motivation to make them happen? Commitment leads to self-discipline, which leads to self-accountability.

If you want to increase commitment, you must:

- *Make your goals achievable.*

- *When your goals are unrealistic, you can't commit to them because you know that they'll be too difficult to achieve.*

- *Make your goals specific.*

- *Goals that are too broad make it difficult to know what steps to take to get there. When goals are unspecific, they can be confusing and this decreases your commitment.*

- *Write your goals down!*

- *What if you have goals in mind but haven't written them down? Remember that those who write down goals achieve more than those who don't. Fourteen percent of people have a goal plan in mind, but these are unwritten goals. Goals 'held' in mind are more likely to be jumbled up with the other 1500 thoughts per minute that the average human being experiences (Matthews, 2019). If you put something on paper, a commitment to that something is much more concrete. If you write your goals on paper, you'll have more loyalty to them than the goals that remain only in your head.*

- *Share your goals with others.*

- *Talking to just one person about your own goal, your commitment will be much more significant than if you are the only person who knows about the goal. Everyone wants to be viewed as a responsible person, even if just in the eyes of the one person you shared your goals with. If you express that you'll do something, there's a higher probability that you will do that thing.*

Janine had committed to raising a specific target of money for the foundation, and in doing so, committed to achieving her goal, no matter what obstacles came her way. She had also shared her goal with countless people, each who helped her raise money. She had specific targets, and she knew that they were achievable, albeit challenging.

Flexibility is the key to success when it comes to achieving goals. There's likely little chance that you will ever create your meaningful future precisely the way you had foreseen it. Instead of viewing this as 'failure', remember that achieving a meaningful goal is a long-distance endurance endeavour. It's a marathon. Or even a triathlon, with many events along the way. You'll learn new things as you go that will require you to change your plan, and that's fine.

The only guarantee is that embarking on the quest towards setting more meaningful goals will take you to new and exciting places. Most importantly, you're more likely to enjoy the journey and embrace the obstacles and victories along the way.

Bibliography

Duckworth, A. (2018). *Grit: The Power of Passion of Perseverance.* New York: Scribner.

Eccles, J.S. & Wigfield, A. (2002). Motivational Beliefs, Values, and Goals. *Annual Review of Psychology* 2002, 53:1, pp. 109–132. Retrieved from https://www.researchgate.net/profile/Jacquelynne_Eccles/publication/281345525_Motivational_Beliefs_Values_and_Goals/links/0c9605162df8d72538000000/Motivational-Beliefs-Values-and-Goals.pdf.

Frankl, V. (1959). *Man's Search for Meaning.* New York: Random House

Frankl, V. (1997). *Recollections: An Autobiography.* New York: Plenum.

Gómez-Miñambres, J. (2012). Motivation through goal setting. *Journal of Economic Psychology*, 33(6), pp. 1223–1239. Retrieved from https://www.sciencedirect.com/science/article/abs/pii/S0167487012000967

Halvorson, H. (2014). *Succeed: How We Can Reach Our Goals.* New York: Plume.

Lyubomirsky, S. (2008). *The How of Happiness.* New York: Penguin Books.

Mathhews, G. (2019). Goals Research Summary. Retrieved December 11, 2019, from https://www.dominican.edu/academics/lae/undergraduate-programs/psych/faculty/assets-gail-matthews/researchsummary2.pdf.

Mitchell, T. R. & Wood, R. E. (1994). Managerial Goal Setting. Journal of Leadership Studies, 1(2), pp. 3–26. Retrieved from https://journals.sagepub.com/doi/abs/10.1177/107179199400100203.

Oettingen, G. (2019) WOOP my life. Retrieved October 1, 2019, from http://woopmylife.org/woop-1 [Accessed 1 Oct. 2019].

2

Creating a Fitness Plan

'A nail is driven out by another nail; habit is overcome by habit.'

Erasmus

Step 2: Choosing workouts that increase your mindset muscle and form new habits

You've committed to a meaningful goal and developed a way to get there. It's time to build your willpower so that you reach your goal and get a podium finish. At the start of this book, I described willpower as motivation and the fuel you need to get to a goal destination. For me, willpower encompasses motivation and self-discipline. Further to this, self-discipline is about the habits we maintain. I also explained how willpower is a mental capability that's part genetic and partly developed through awareness. To build awareness about your willpower, it's crucial to understand how willpower works.

Before I get into the science, I'd like to tell you about Kirsten Naude.

I've known Kirsten since I was a child living in South Africa, and though we haven't lived in the same country for two decades, I've admired Kirsten's achievements throughout our lives. My fondest childhood memory of Kirsten is her talent as a musician. Her ability to play the piano always filled me with awe, and her vocal talents always left me speechless. As adults, Kirsten's professional achievements are equally inspiring to me. Today, Kirsten lives in the UK and has the title of 'Director'. She owns her own business and is also part of the senior leadership team at a large children's charity. Kirsten's passion is to help charities and social enterprises explore new ways to both innovate and find better and more impactful ways to help their beneficiaries. She also helps them generate greater support for their causes, which might be in the form of money, time or developing voice.

Three years ago, Kirsten decided to establish her own business so that she could use her skills to help organisations be better at what they do. She had a dream to drive change in the charity sector so that they benefit the people they could serve transparently and authentically.

Kirsten achieved quicker than she expected. Following setting up her business, she immediately secured two contracts, and she's never had to tender or bid for a piece of work since. She has repeat business and clients returning to her for help with new projects, which she says is the greatest achievement of all. She's done this while maintaining her full-time director role in the charity she works for.

I was interested to know what kind of habits Kirsten has. She gave me a fantastic list.

Her first habit is to use her 'design thinking' knowledge, which has helped her build a 'just do it' mindset. She went on to say: 'You won't truly know whether something is good or not until you try it. The proof is in the pudding. Failure isn't a bad thing – I see it more as a learning experience – not one that should keep you hosting a perpetual pity party.'

Kirsten also says time management is a crucial habit. In the first few months of running her business, and taking on two new clients with chunky briefs, she was also managing a full-time job, but she nearly burned out. Now she's more careful about what work she takes on, how she phrases it, and how it aligns with all of the other activities going on in her life – both socially and professionally.

Probably the most interesting habit that Kirsten mentioned was that she only works on something when she 'feels it'.

She describes it this way: 'Sometimes working on a specific project, report, or big piece of work is draining and downright excruciating. It feels like a mountain that won't move. I think it's so important to "be in the zone" when tackling this type of work. What I mean by this is being in the right headspace, armed with the right tools and energy levels to plough through it. You can waste so much time and energy, forcing yourself to work when you're not in a groove or in the headspace to do so. I used to feel guilty, putting off large work challenges.'

'I'd always felt bad for leaving it and doing it when I felt abler. I thought I'd never get to it. Time and time again, I've proven that the time does come when my mind shifts a gear and I'm ready to tackle the work. Where deadlines loom, it might not always be possible to work in this way, but for the most part, it's proven more efficient and effective for me.'

Kirsten says this habit has been transformational in helping her achieve goals in her life. I asked Kirsten how else she keeps herself motivated. She explained that whenever she loses her motivation, she'll always 'talk it out' with her most trusted advisors who act as her sounding board. They will be different people for different things. Some advice is about practice and approach; other times, she can rant and air her emotions. She's also very connected to her parents. She describes them as her biggest cheerleaders and is grateful to have them around. 'Even when I'm doing everything wrong, they have a special way of helping me see the silver lining,' Kirsten says. Her valuable advice for motivation is to have a network of support that you can both draw on, and give to.

Kirsten also ensures she regularly returns to her South African roots to keep her grounded. She says that it's a source of replenishment for her and reminds her why she does what she does.

Kirsten says, 'Giving, especially of my time, my listening ear and my skills, has always been a good way to shift the focus away from "all things self" and onto helping others. This helps balance me out.'

Similarly, going on a holiday to places where she can broaden her horizons and learn new things leaves her full of creativity and new ideas. And she gets extra thinking time!

Lastly, Kirsten makes sure she exercises. This allows her to release stress, gives her some 'alone' thinking time and promotes positive mental health and wellbeing. Kirsten says it's easy for negativity to creep in both physically and mentally when she doesn't exercise.

Kirsten gave me many pearls of wisdom in her correspondence with me. Here are her top tips for achieving your goals:

- *Ensure that you surround yourself with genuine supporters – people who've got your back and who will be honest with you. We aren't able to see our blindspots – have someone pointing those out (although hard to hear sometimes) will help you avoid a world of pain in the long run.*

- *Self-care is so important. Don't ever sacrifice your mental health to meet unrealistic expectations from yourself or those from others. Make sure you take sufficient time out to rest – to sleep – and to enjoy activities that help de-stress and bring a sense of joy and wellbeing. Cognitive behavioural therapy training worked wonders for Kirsten, and she still uses all the techniques she learned. Understand your body's red flags, and know when enough is enough – learn to say no.*

- *Build goodwill as capital. Try not to burn bridges, as tempting as it might be in some situations. It can be super helpful when calling in a favour. You never know what the future holds – some relationships will surprise you and bring to light opportunities you never expected.*

- *Honesty is a powerful tool. Being open about how you're doing, how you're feeling, and what you're going through (without relaying your life story in one go), can be very helpful to others. People are not mind-readers. They don't know what you're going through and can't support you adequately unless you tell them. Kirsten says, 'Taking this approach has helped me connect with people on a more empathic and personal level. Don't ever underestimate the power of a trust relationship.'*

Kirsten's final words truly sum up her ability to motivate herself and stay disciplined in her pursuits: 'I now believe that anything is possible; I just need to give it a whirl and see where I end up. I might end up in a very different place to where I envisaged being at the start – but I still moved. And that's the most important thing.'

Keep Kirsten's story in mind as we explore willpower and how it works.

The science of willpower

Psychologist Roy Baumeister made an exciting discovery about willpower in 1998. He found that people who were forced to exert willpower by resisting eating cookies placed in front of them did worse on subsequent puzzles and problem-solving tasks than people who indulged themselves with the cookies beforehand (Baumeister et al., 1998). Researchers thought this might have been an accident, and so they retested this using many different scenarios with the same result.

Willpower is depleted as it's used up. Let's think of that using the fuel tank analogy from earlier. If you fill up your fuel tank then drive all day without topping up the tank, you're going to run out of fuel. If you later decide to go to a new destination on the map, you're not going to have enough fuel to get you there.

Once we use up all our willpower, we're far more prone to give up. This phenomenon is referred to as 'ego depletion' (Baumeister et al., 1998). Before you think you've never experienced ego depletion, let me ask you this: Have you ever gotten home from a long and challenging day at work and had no motivation to cook dinner or go to the gym?

So if our willpower is finite, how is it possible to achieve anything new on top of what we're already doing? We can look at Kirsten's story as an example of how it is possible. She didn't deplete her willpower fuel tanks while setting up her new business, although she says she came close to it at one point. That's because willpower can be made stronger. It can also be weakened and atrophied (Mischel et al., 2010). Willpower can be built up over some time by consistently accomplishing a series of tasks. You get used to using the willpower, and your fuel is used up more slowly. You essentially burn fuel more efficiently. It's the same as going from being able to run 5 km to being able to run 42 km. You build up your strength and endurance over time, through consistent training and gradual increases of distance each week. Soon enough, running 10 km is easy, where that same distance a few weeks before would have been challenging. You never just start running a marathon distance without the proper training. It's the same with willpower.

Stronger willpower is why Kirsten can focus and work through 10-hour days as a director of a charity, hit the gym and then go home then work on her own business. Kirsten isn't more extraordinary than you or I. She's practised willpower enough to make that level of productivity her new normal. And she even admits that her fuel tank can run on empty sometimes. Her habits help her to keep her fuel tank topped up.

This brings me back to the mental marathons I discussed at the start of this book. At some point, you will be required to take part in challenges, either personally or professionally, that will require a lot of motivation and discipline. If your willpower is depleted before you get to the podium, you're going to struggle.

How does the Mindset Fitness Program increase willpower?

If you want to build your willpower muscles, you have to set and accomplish tasks. That's where the Mindset Fitness Workouts come in. The workouts in this book provide double benefits. First, they require some willpower to complete each day. They won't deplete your fuel tank, but instead, they'll help you install a larger, more efficient one. Second, the workouts themselves serve specific goals for improving your mindset. So not only will your mindset develop so that you achieve your goals, you'll strengthen your willpower so you won't burn out.

This part of the Mindset Fitness Program goes hand in hand with setting the meaningful goals from Chapter 1.

Here's an example of why: Many people set goals to lose weight at one time or other in their life. They usually take a willpower-only approach. They pick a random weight loss goal – such as to lose 5 kg in 2 months – and then they starve themselves or exercise furiously for a few weeks. They believe that if they have the willpower to turn away from cookies after dinner every day, then they'll achieve their goal. Or perhaps they'll start jogging when they hate jogging. They believe that by torturing themselves that they'll lose the 5 kg, and be happy. What happens with most people eventually is that they experience ego depletion. Their willpower fuel disappears, and soon enough, they reach for a cookie, or stop jogging altogether.

A different approach would be to set a meaningful goal, as described in Chapter 1. For example, instead of losing 5 kg, your goal is rather to improve your health so that you can play with your children more or live longer with your grandchildren. You then create a series of habits that, over time, install a larger fuel tank.

Research has found that about 43% of our behaviour may be habitual. When taking a look at 'experience sampling' research, people recorded once per hour what they were thinking, feeling, and doing and about 43% of those actions were performed almost daily and usually in the same context (Wood et al., 2002). So if you approach your meaningful goal with a series of habits, you start to choose healthier meal options because you enjoy the food and it isn't a source of self-discipline anymore. You take up a water aerobics class because it's fun rather than force yourself to jog. Soon enough, you may find that the 5 kg is ultimately lost. This time, however, you've developed a series of habits that support your meaningful goal, and you've installed a larger fuel tank.

Following the Mindset Fitness Program helps you exert your willpower on making changes that are sustainable, rather than using all your effort making choices that you'll give up on eventually. By reading Kirsten's story, are you able to identify her meaningful goal and how she used habits to support her achievements?

It's simple to make the right decisions based on willpower for a short period. But as is the case in many goal-setting situations, people run out of willpower and cave in to their previous habits.

In the book *Atomic Habits* by James Clear (2018), he states that success is the product of daily habits – not once-in-a-lifetime transformations. He goes on to say, 'With outcome-based habits, the focus is on what you want to achieve (lose 5 kg). With identity-based habits, the focus is on whom you wish to become (a fit and healthy grandparent).'

Do you think Kirsten forces herself into making daily decisions to run her business while working full time, all the while internally resisting it? Of course not! She would have depleted her willpower fuel tank a long time ago. She'd have burned herself out in less than a week. Research has shown that people who set numerous and simultaneous goals end up accomplishing none of them. They suffer high levels of burnout and never turn any goal into a habit (Dalton and Spiller, 2012). Kirsten mentioned how she changed her approach so that she could focus on fewer competing priorities at a time. Focusing on single goals and building up to them slowly over extended periods by implementing habits is far more effective.

Develop habits

To increase your mindset fitness, you'll have to develop a series of habits and choose daily workouts. These should take no more than 5–10 minutes per day and should happen at the most productive time of the day for you. By practicing the willpower required to commit to the Mindset Fitness Workouts, you'll also develop the willpower to achieve your goals.

Research from Wood and Neal (2007) found that goals can direct habits by motivating repetition that leads to habit formation and by promoting exposure to cues that trigger habits. After something becomes a habit, our behaviour isn't guided by our internal goals and motivations anymore. 'Once a habit is formed, the perception of contexts triggers the associated response without a mediating goal.' (Wood & Neal, 2007).

In the book *The Power of Habit* by Charles Duhigg (2013), he summarises research on how habits are created, broken, and maintained. Studies show that habits are comprised of three parts: an environmental cue, a behavioural response, and a reward. Habits are the automatic behavioural responses we have to cues in our environment. Cues can be familiar situations, or people, or events. We can keep our goals in mind and then consciously use our willpower to manipulate our situations and develop habits to the cues of our choosing. In this way, we can leverage everything around us to create automatic, habitual behaviours that will help us to reach our goals.

Let's say you have a habit of regularly checking your phone messages or social media accounts. The cue is the notification sound or icon. The behaviour response is checking your phone. The reward is reading a message.

The cue triggers your craving to perform the habit of checking your messages. You check the message, and you feel more relaxed. If you decided to stop this habit, you may find that you'd spend your time and willpower on creating or eliminating the behaviour itself (that is, stop picking up the phone when you get a notification). Instead, you should consciously create and reorganise the cues in your environment that trigger those habits. Researchers have found that to develop new habits (or break old habits), we should focus on what the cues are, rather than focus on the behaviour (Duhigg, 2014). A better approach would be to silence those notification alerts, rather than resisting the urge to check the message.

So, using the workouts in this book as an example, instead of focusing on developing the habit of 'doing the workout', focus on developing a routine around initiating a workout.

A simple way to do this is to choose a cue that already occurs regularly in your day. An example would be reading a book in bed before you sleep. A workout example would be practising gratitude. Now, during the early stages of developing your workout habit, focus your effort on climbing into bed, and before you start reading, think of all the things that happened that day for which you are grateful. You develop the habit of putting yourself in the position to practise gratitude regularly, which makes it more likely that you'll *do* the exercise. This is sometimes called 'habit stacking'. It's where you add a habit to a habit you already have (Clear, 2018).

After a while, you'll start noticing that when you get to climb into bed, it's not difficult to reflect on the day and practise gratitude. You may begin to look forward to it, and maybe also feel like something in your life is off when you don't do the workout.

So how long does this take? There's a persistent myth that it takes 30 days or 30 repetitions to create a habit. Research shows that our brains don't add up the repetitive behaviour, reach a threshold of repetitions, and then treat it as an automatic habit. Instead, habits are formed gradually and over time (Clear, 2018).

Here's how it works.

At first, regularly repeating a behaviour causes a quick increase in how habitual it is. Initially, the response is not at all automatic, so time will have an impact on making it so. After repeated practise, your brain gradually forms a new habit in response to a cue, but it doesn't just suddenly happen after a set number of repetitions. It's like a dimmer switch – the more you turn the switch, the brighter the light burns.

Choosing workouts that support good habits

Knowing the basics of how habits work can significantly increase your chances of developing good habits. Merely by reading something like this book gives you a leg up on establishing healthy habits in your life (Tice et al., 2007). All you need to do is choose what works for you.

However, studies suggest that having too much choice and choosing between options is more depleting than merely deliberating and forming preferences about options (Vohs et al., 2008). Therefore, I have only twelve workouts in this book – three workouts per mindset theme. The Mindset Fitness Program can be seen as a whole in the diagram at the start of this section of the book. The themes are flexibility, strength, endurance and composition. Working on a combination of themes has a different outcome. My suggestion is that you read through each theme and decide which areas of your mindset that you need to strengthen. From there, you can develop a program of workouts tailored to your needs.

Another factor in improving your ability to build good habits is the perception of the habit you're trying to create. If the habit seems too impossible, then it will be harder to form. If it looks natural or straightforward, then it will be more comfortable (Duhigg, 2014). The mindset workouts in this book are designed to be comfortable and feel natural.

And once you've mastered an easy habit, you can always ramp it up to a more complex one.

For example, one of the workouts in this book is to practise gratitude. Find five things to be grateful for each day, and it becomes easy over time. Then you may not find it so difficult to start thinking of ten things per day that you're thankful for. Later, you can try finding gratitude moments throughout your day rather in just one hit. You may eventually find that you fill your day with gratitude without even thinking about it. This would have seemed impossible at first.

While consistency is important, research has shown that missing a handful of opportunities to practise a new habit will not be detrimental to forming a habit in the long run. Don't be too hard on yourself for missing a workout session. Merely acknowledge that this is how habits work and continue with your routine as soon as you can.

Further, you don't need to do all the workouts every day. It's better to do a small amount often rather than a long session infrequently or on weekends. Choose one or two focus workouts to practise daily and for a while. Develop these as habits and practise habit stacking alongside cues. Each workout shouldn't take longer than 10 minutes to complete, making it pretty easy to include this alongside other existing rituals and habits. Instead of setting a goal of doing 3 hours of workouts each night, expend your willpower on habits that will make that mindset inevitable in the long term.

When to do the workouts

Further to developing habits alongside a cue as mentioned earlier, there are also ideal times of day that allow you to focus better.

In his 2018 book *When: The Scientific Secrets of Perfect Timing*, Daniel Pink references psychological, biological and economic studies to explore the overlooked element of timing in our habit-forming. Pink found that timing exerts an enormous effect on what we do and how we do it. He shares some tremendous hacks to optimise your life. He says, 'We all know timing is everything; the trouble is we don't know much about timing itself.'

There's a pattern each of us follows every day. We naturally think of our days in three parts: morning, afternoon, and evening. Humans have lived with this pattern for hundreds or thousands of years. However, we can spot a subtler pattern lying over those three parts that have to do with our emotions.

A study by Cornell University analysed 500 million tweets on Twitter and found that during the morning people peak. Either immediately after waking up or 1–2 hours later, most people feel good earlier in the day. Then in the afternoon, people experience an emotional trough. You know how it's tough to stay awake or motivated after lunch? That's the afternoon trough. And then in the evening, people experience a rebound – that feeling you get when you finish work, and you suddenly have more energy (Pink, 2018).

This happens no matter what age you are, what your race is, what gender you are, or what your nationality is. Daniel Kahneman, the author of *Thinking Fast and Slow*, confirmed this with the Day Reconstruction Method (DRM). These findings have implications for how we should structure our days and it's also an excellent pattern to be aware of to deal with your emotions more efficiently (Kahneman, 2013).

We can learn much about ourselves if we combine this knowledge of our emotional cycles with our circadian rhythm. Eventually, we come to some insight as to when our highs and lows occur during the day.

Some people say that they can't wake up before 7 am. Others say they are night owls, while others (like me) love to get up early. We often dismiss those sentiments as people not being used to certain behaviours (like waking up early), but science says there's some truth to it. Your feelings during certain times of day belong to one of three chronotypes, as described by Pink:

The Lark: These are people like me, who love to wake up early, and have all their emotional highs and lows and work done before noon. Don't ask me to do anything at 9 pm; I'm probably asleep on the couch.

The Owl: These are people who don't like getting up early, will sleep until noon if you let them, and can start work on complex problems around 9 pm. My partner Josh is an owl. Josh slowly wakes up in the morning, and by the afternoon, he's only just starting to get up to speed.

The Third Bird: This is the majority of people around you. They are neither late nor early risers and follow the standard pattern of the morning, afternoon and evening.

Third birds should do analytical, logic-based work in the mornings when they're most alert. They should do more creative tasks, where it's helpful if their mind wanders, later in the afternoon.

Larks can follow the same pattern but only a couple of hours earlier in the day. Owls should do the cognitive work late at night and the creative stuff in the morning. Whatever your type, you have one thing in common: doing boring admin stuff in the afternoon trough is always a good idea!

What does this mean for your mindset workouts? Choosing more creative and fun workouts should be done in the times when your mind wanders, and the more analytical tasks should be done in your alert times.

In the course of completing the Mindset Fitness Program, you'll first need to develop a routine and then form a habit of doing the workouts. A routine is a behaviour frequently repeated. Unlike a habit, skipping a routine doesn't feel bad and without proper forethought, can be easily skipped or forgotten. So initially, while you bring the workouts into your routine, it may be easy to skip a few. Lucky for us, missing one opportunity to perform the behaviour doesn't affect the habit formation process (Lally et al., 2009).

Some routines can become habits, but only if it's a behaviour that can be done with little conscious thought. Trying to turn a behaviour that requires a lot of effort into a habit will backfire if you expect it to be effortless quickly. Forming a habit requires sticking to a routine. Make time in your schedule, and link it to a cue you already have. Expect and learn to cope with discomfort, and find ways to pre-commit to the task.

Chapter 5 through to Chapter 8 describe the mindset themes in more detail and give you workouts to choose from. I urge you to come back to Kirsten's story to find common ideas in her habits and suggestions. For now, let's explore what you'll do after you've achieved your podium finish and are ready to choose your next race.

Bibliography

Baumeister, R. F., Bratslavsky, E., Muraven, M. & Tice, D. M. (1998). Ego depletion: is the active self a limited resource? *Journal of Personality and Social Psychology*, 74(5), pp. 1252. Retrieved from https://psycnet.apa.org/doiLanding?doi=10.1037/0022-3514.74.5.1252.

Clear, J. (2018). *Atomic Habits: Tiny Changes, Remarkable Results: an Easy & Proven Way to Build Good Habits & Break Bad Ones.* New York: Avery.

Dalton, A. & Spiller, S. (2012). Too Much of a Good Thing: The Benefits of Implementation Intentions Depend on the Number of Goals. *Journal of Consumer Research*, 39(3), pp. 600–614. Retrieved from https://academic.oup.com/jcr/article-abstract/39/3/600/1822636.

Duhigg, C. (2014). *The Power of Habit.* USA: Random House.

Kahneman, D. (2013). *Thinking, Fast and Slow.* New York: Farrar, Straus and Giroux.

Lally, P., Van Jaarsveld, C. H., Potts, H. W. & Wardle, J. (2010). How are habits formed: Modeling habit formation in the real world. *European Journal of Social Psychology*, 40(6), pp. 998–1009. Retrieved from https://onlinelibrary.wiley.com/doi/abs/10.1002/ejsp.674.

Mischel, W., Ayduk, O., Berman, M., Casey, B., Gotlib, I., Jonides, J., Kross, E., Teslovich, T., Wilson, N., Zayas, V. & Shoda, Y. (2010). 'Willpower' over the life span: decomposing self-regulation. *Social Cognitive and Affective Neuroscience*, 6(2), pp. 252–256. Retrieved from https://academic.oup.com/scan/article/6/2/252/1619382.

Pink, D. (2018). *When.* New York: Random House.

Tice, D. M., Baumeister, R. F., Shmueli, D. & Muraven, M. (2007). Restoring the self: Positive affect helps improve self-regulation following ego depletion. *Journal of Experimental Social Psychology*, 43(3), pp. 379–384. Retrieved from https://www.sciencedirect.com/science/article/abs/pii/S0022103106000862.

Vohs, K., Baumeister, R., Schmeichel, B., Twenge, J., Nelson, N. & Tice, D. (2008). Making choices impairs subsequent self-control: A limited-resource account of decision making, self-regulation, and active initiative. *Journal of Personality and Social Psychology*, 94(5), pp. 883–898. Retrieved from https://www.taylorfrancis.com/books/e/9781315175775/chapters/10.4324/9781315175775-2.

Wood, W. & Neal, D. (2007). A new look at habits and the habit-goal interface. *Psychological Review*, 114(4), pp. 843–863. Retrieved from https://psycnet.apa.org/record/2007-13558-001.

Wood, W., Quinn, J. & Kashy, D. (2002). Habits in everyday life: Thought, emotion, and action. *Journal of Personality and Social Psychology*, 83(6), pp. 1281–1297. Retrieved from https://psycnet.apa.org/record/2002-08203-004.

3

Getting a Podium Finish

'Burnout is nature's way of telling you you've been going through the motions your soul has departed; you're a zombie, a member of the walking dead, a sleepwalker. False optimism is like administrating stimulants to an exhausted nervous system.'

Sam Keen, Fire in the Belly: On Being a Man

Step 3: Achieving results without burning out

At this stage of the Mindset Fitness Program, you're now diligently working towards your goal while practising workouts to increase your chances of success. As discussed in previous chapters, we need the 'way power' to achieve our goals and the willpower to stay on course. We also know that willpower is finite, and that it can be built and practised. So what happens when you don't exercise your willpower muscles and keep your mindset fit for success? The short answer is that you burn out. You deplete your tank, and soon enough, you no longer have the energy to continue to reach your goal. If you want to achieve results, you must recognise and prevent burnout.

Kelli Pickford is a British-born Australian who set out to relocate to Australia with her partner and young family a few years ago. It was a meaningful goal for Kelli because of the lifestyle change the move would provide and the opportunities her young daughter would have. It wasn't an easy decision for Kelli and pursuing the goal often brought Kelli close to burnout. She was juggling being a new mum, a busy work schedule and the severe illness of three family members over a short period. Those are a lot of competing priorities. Kelli soon felt a lack of clarity of thinking and became short-tempered and overly sensitive. She started to lack confidence in her decisions, began to hesitate, and felt overwhelmed.

When I asked Kelli what she did to help herself with this and prevent burning out completely, she said:

'There were four main things. First, running helped me clear my head and gain some clarity. I would also stay in the moment for a while. It is difficult to be in those situations. Still, I needed to experience the emotions rather than trying to plan a way forward without having a clear pathway. I would remind myself that I would get through this, even though it was difficult, I knew it wouldn't always be that way, and I need to trust the process. And I also made sure I had some wine and good friends available.'

Kelli did achieve her goal, and she ended up in Australia in one piece. Even though it was difficult to consider leaving family during those difficult times, she stayed focused on the lifestyle she wanted in Australia. As a side note – Kelli later entered and completed her first triathlon in Australia.

Kelli says that the best advice she can give to others is to not to be afraid of big goals and not settle for the status quo just because something is difficult. She also says to be clear on a vision and move towards it but to not over plan the journey. She says if you 'plan the outcomes' you won't be disappointed.

What is burnout?

The *Journal of Applied Biobehavioral Research* published an article citing that burnout is having a growing impact in populations of advanced economies, and can have economic impacts (Proshkina, 2019). Further, a Gallup study of nearly 7500 full-time employees in 2018 found that 23% always reported (or very often reported) feeling burned out, while an additional 44% reported feeling burned out sometimes.

Burnout is characterised by ineffectiveness, chronic negative responses and emotional exhaustion. It occurs when you feel unable to meet the constant demands of your work or home life are feel emotionally drained (Kaschka et al., 2011). If the stress continues, you begin to lose the interest in activities that previously excited, you and eventually all your motivation. I mentioned the mental marathons we're all required to participate in at certain times in our lives. I look at Kelli's story and see the mental marathon she was running with family, work and goal pressures. Burnout is essentially the mental exhaustion that comes with running these marathons continuously over time.

In the same way that running 42 km can sap all your energy before you cross the finish line, burnout reduces productivity. It leaves you feeling increasingly resentful, hopeless, and cynical. Eventually, you have no more energy left to keep going. The effects of this penetrate every area of your life. You become less sociable, more cynical with family members and colleagues, and it can make you vulnerable to illnesses like colds and flu. Burnout is not just work-related. People caring for children or elderly parents can also experience this type of extreme exhaustion (Kaschka et al., 2011).

The reasons why this happens are complex. One way to see why it happens is to understand that we use mental models to help us navigate situations. A mental model is a way your brain tells you how something works. It's a worldview that you carry around in your mind to help you interpret the world and understand the relationship between things. Mental models provide rational solutions and ideas for how we navigate our environment. They help us stay focused during periods of uncertainty because they give us answers for navigating the changes we experience. If our mental models and reality don't match, we update our models with new information.

Neuroscientists call this process of continually updating mental models 'reflective learning'. We experience something new, we learn, and then creatively update our mental models. It's critical for survival because it allows us to plan our actions and better understand their outcomes. This type of learning is also called goal-directed learning because we're constantly scanning our environment and seeking new learning opportunities. It helps us renew our mental models. We also automatically match our memories to current experiences. If our memories don't match our experiences, we experience novelty – and novelty creates personal growth (Held et al., 2006).

However, if we cannot focus our attention using a mental model or the mental model becomes defunct, we experience cognitive exhaustion. Cognitive exhaustion occurs when we repeatedly fail to find solutions to problems (Held et al., 2006). When we stop being creative and stop making new mental models, we enter a state of 'learned helplessness'. This phenomenon was first described by the father of positive psychology, Martin Seligman, who observed that dogs exposed to inescapable electric shocks demonstrated performance deficits in subsequent learning tasks. The same dogs also lost hope, so that when they were given a solution to escape the shocks, they just allowed themselves to be continually shocked (Seligman, 1970).

In effect, when we're in stressful situations and continuously fail to find solutions, we become overloaded. This overload creates a feeling of helplessness that's difficult to escape. This is burnout.

Are stress and burnout the same?

Burnout is the result of unrelenting stress and cognitive exhaustion, but it isn't the same as experiencing too much stress. Stress demands much of you physically and mentally. But stressed people can still imagine solutions, and feel that once they get control of the situation they'll no longer feel stressed. Feelings of stress equates to 'too much pressure'. Kelli's story illustrates this for us. She was experiencing high levels of stress and that could have easily led to burnout. Thankfully, she had several positive strategies to prevent this.

Burnout is different. Burnout creates a feeling of 'I don't have enough'. Burned-out people feel empty and exhausted. They're often beyond caring about what will happen in the future and don't foresee a positive change. Excessive stress feels like you're drowning, while burnout feels like you're hanging out to dry. And you probably don't even know you're burning out.

It must also be said that there is an optimal level of stress. Chapter 4 goes into more detail about comfort zones. The diagram below illustrates that there's a zone of stress where we are motivated and stimulated to keep working and create solutions. Burnout occurs when we're overstimulated for too long. And comfort zones may eventually understimulate us and creates boredom.

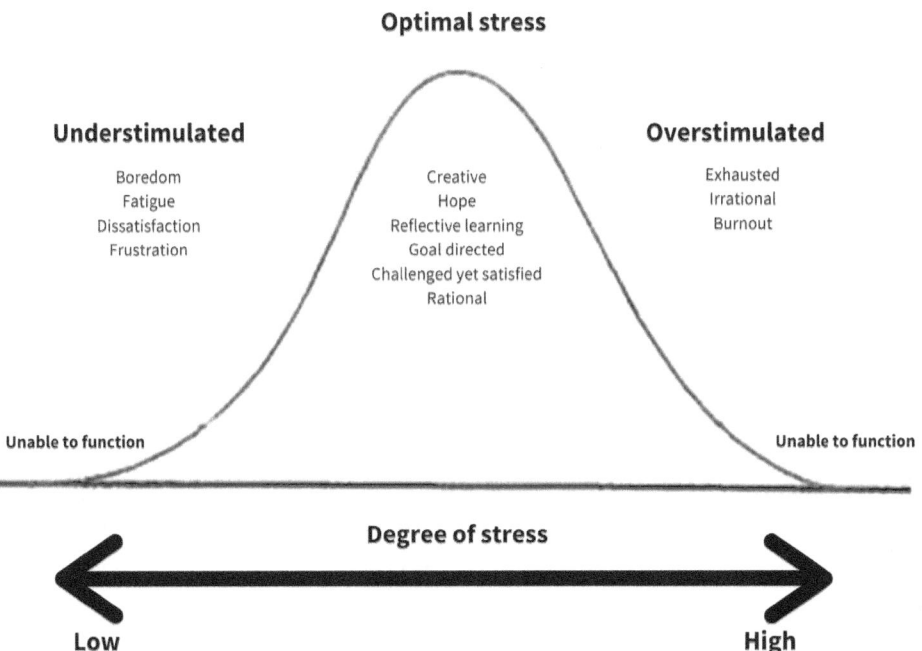

Anyone who feels like they have too much to do while feeling undervalued is at risk of experiencing burnout. But it's not caused solely by stressful work or too many responsibilities. Factors such as personality traits, mindset, and lifestyle also contribute. How you look at the world and what you do to relax can play a significant role in causing overwhelming stress.

Workplace causes of burnout

Well-known leadership and workplace author Jeffrey Pfeffer talks about stress and burnout in his book *Dying for a Paycheck*. In it, he says that workplace burnout costs the USA an estimated $300 billion in healthcare spending each year. It's linked to type 2 diabetes, coronary heart disease, gastrointestinal issues, high cholesterol and even death for those under the age of 45. In China, one million people a year may be dying from being overworked (Pfeffer, 2018).

Workplace burnout occurs when you feel you have little or no control over your work and don't feel like you're recognised for that work. Monotony or a lack of novelty also contributes. There are higher instances of burnout when there's little clarity and overly demanding expectations in a chaotic environment. And when work is the only meaningful activity in your life, you also may experience burnout (Kaschka et al., 2011). Can you see the importance of proper goal-setting now? If you're reading this as a leader of a team, you should also see the importance of helping your team set the right goals and manage their stress.

Lifestyle causes of burnout

Your lifestyle can contribute to burnout. This may all seem obvious to you. People who work long hours without enough time for socialising or relaxing are more likely to burn out over time, especially if they don't get enough sleep. Those with few supportive relationships also experience burnout more often (Kaschka et al., 2011). Kelli showed us how the strategy of maintaining her social connections was an essential part of preventing burnout for her. If you're one of those people who hates to ask for help, you're at risk of burning out.

Personality and mindset traits that cause burnout

Perfectionists are people who try to make everything line up perfectly. They struggle to finish tasks because the task never feels 100% complete and right. Nothing is ever good enough for a perfectionist, and as a result, they're more likely to burn out than someone who isn't (Kaschka et al., 2011).

Those with a pessimistic view of themselves and the world around them also experience burnout. They're more likely to feel helpless and hopeless. Kelli's example shows us how she had a hopeful view of the world and knew that her difficulties would end. High achievers are also at risk, especially if they always want to please other people and suppress their own needs. They have an extrinsic view of the world and don't set intrinsic goals. Kelli's goals were indeed meaningful to her. They were about her intrinsic needs, rather than about pleasing everyone around her. Lastly, those who need to maintain control and fail to delegate tasks are also more likely to burn out.

The warning signs and why the Mindset Fitness Workout helps

Psychologists Herbert Freudenberger and Gail North published research on burnout in 1992 and identified twelve phases of burnout syndrome (Ponocny-Seliger & Winker, 2014). These are handy to know because if you recognise any of the signs, you should consider putting a prevention plan in place. The phases are:

1. **Excessive drive/ambition:** *This is especially common for people starting a new job or undertaking a new task; too much ambition can lead to burnout.*

2. **Ambition pushes you to work harder:** *You don't want to let anyone down.*

3. **Neglecting your own needs:** *You may sacrifice self-care like sleep, exercise, and eating well. Kelli recognised that exercise was an important part of keeping stress levels under control.*

4. **Displacement of conflict:** *Instead of acknowledging your contribution to the problem, you blame everyone and everything around you for your troubles.*

5. **No time for non work-related needs:** *You begin to withdraw from family and friends.*

6. **Denial:** *Impatience with those around you mounts. Kelli showed this symptom when she became overly sensitive with those around her. You continue to blame others, seeing them as incompetent, lazy and overbearing.*

7. **Withdrawal:** *You begin to entirely withdraw from family, friends and social invitations because they feel burdensome.*

8. **Behavioural changes:** *You become snappy and more aggressive towards friends and loved ones.*

9. **Depersonalisation:** *You start to feel detached from your life and your ability to control your life.*

10. **Inner emptiness or anxiety:** *You may turn to thrill-seeking or addiction behaviours to cope*

11. **Depression:** *You begin to feel hopeless, and things start to lose meaning.*

12. **Mental or physical collapse:** *Medical or mental health attention may be necessary.*

The Mindset Fitness Workout provides solutions to many of these phases of burnout. It helps you set meaningful goals that are not extrinsic so that your drive and ambition is not misplaced. It encourages you to look after your personal needs and increases your ability to reflect and put things into the proper perspective. And the Mindset Fitness Workout also encourages you to ask for help and maintain social connections while improving your ability to reflect and chunk down goals so that you feel more in control.

The road to burnout leaves you feeling helpless, but there are positive steps you can take to deal with the causes of stress and burnout and get yourself back into a state of balance. You can learn how to prevent burnout and feel healthy and positive (Awa, Plaumann and Walter, 2010). The workouts in this book are designed to give you the way power and the willpower to succeed. They will increase your ability to maintain good habits, and they will decrease burnout because they decrease negative thinking traps that create stress, and this improves your mindset. I hope that by reading this book you will pause and change direction, and get into the habit of working out your mindset.

The Mindset Fitness Workout means avoiding the mindless persistence towards a goal without assessing if you're tired or need to adjust. Getting a podium finish means staying fit, healthy and aware. Don't expect immediate results. The workouts must be done consistently and with diligence. In that way, you will increase your willpower and way power to go the distance with your goal. This is what Step 3 is about – continuing to exercise your mindset so that you achieve results and prevent burnout.

If you recognise a few of the warning signs or you're already past the breaking point, I urge you to not push through the exhaustion. Continuing will only cause further emotional and physical damage. If this is the case, I urge you to seek support and manage stress.

Bibliography

Awa, W., Plaumann, M. & Walter, U. (2010). Burnout prevention: A review of intervention programs. *Patient Education and Counseling.* 78(2), pp. 184–190. Retrieved from https://www.sciencedirect.com/science/article/pii/S0738399109001621.

Gallup, I. (2019). Employee Burnout, Part 1: The 5 Main Causes. Retrieved October 12, 2019, from https://www.gallup.com/workplace/237059/employee-burnout-part-main-causes.aspx.

Held, C., Knau, M., Vosgerau, G. & Johnson-Laird, P. (2006). *Mental Models in Cognitive Psychology.* Neuroscience, and Philosophy of Mind 1. Amsterdam: Elsevier.

Kaschka W. P., Korczak D. & Broich K. (2011). Burnout: a fashionable diagnosis. *Deutsches Ärzteblatt International*, 108, pp. 781–797. Retrieved from https://www.ncbi.nlm.nih.gov/pmc/articles/PMC3230825.

Pfeffer, J. (2018). *Dying for a Paycheck: How Modern Management Harms Employee Health and Company Performance – and What We Can Do About It.* New York: Harper Collins

Ponocny-Seliger E. & Winker R. (2014). 12-phase burnout screening, development, implementation and test theoretical analysis of a burnout screening based on the 12-phase model of Herbert Freudenberger and Gail North. ASU Int. 2014;, 49, pp. 927–935.

Seligman, M. E. P. (1970). Nontransient learned helplessness. *Psychonomic Science*, 19, pp. 191–192. Retrieved from https://link.springer.com/article/10.3758/BF03335546.

Vladimirovna Proshkina, O. & Ilinichna Efremova, O. (2019). The Cyclical Phenomenon of the Burnout Syndrome, Research in Applied Linguistics, 10 (Proceedings of the 6th International Conference on Applied Linguistics Issues (ALI 2019) July 19–20, 2019, Saint Petersburg, Russia), pp. 694–702.

4

Signing Up for the Next Race

'As you move outside of your comfort zone, what was once the unknown and frightening becomes your new normal.'

Robin S Sharma

Step 4: Choosing your next goals

Allan Donaldson is the head coach of the South African national drum majorettes team. He's also the coach of St Dominic's drum majorette team and has been since he was 19-years-old (in 1976). Also, Allan is the owner of a sports-related business called Allan Donaldson Promotions. He's the founder and chairman of both the South African Drum Majorette and Cheerleading and Association (1981) and the Gauteng Majorette and Cheerleading Association (1979).

Having been involved in the pipe band world throughout his school years, he was asked to become the coach of St Dominic's drum majorettes in 1976. The team entered its first competition under his guidance shortly after that and managed an excellent second placing behind the South African champion team at the time.

Life as a coach seemed easy for Allan, but he soon discovered this was not the case. A few weeks later, while he was away at a pipe band competition as the pipe major, St Dominic's only achieved 13th place at their second competition. On hearing this news, Allan resolved to make St Dominic's the best drum majorette team in the world. Not a small goal!

That same evening he gave up his pipe band life, and set out to achieve this audacious new goal. He'd realised that he had a deep-rooted passion for the sport, the girls in the team and what being a member of a successful team could mean to those girls in their future lives.

This goal took Allan far out of his comfort zone. While he had loads of experience in pipe bands and been a drill instructor in the South African defence force, he'd never been a teacher or coach, and more importantly, had never coached girls. He wanted to achieve the best for them and to show them that hard work and perseverance always pays off, and to show them that if you start something and put the time and effort into it, you can achieve great heights. He didn't want the team to think of themselves as members of a school extracurricular activity, but instead to commit fully and to the best of their ability.

Initially, Allan wanted to achieve competition victories but soon came to realise that the mere collection of medals and trophies was not enough. So the goal of winning, while never going away, evolved into the more important goal of passing on the values of doing things for the right reasons, hard work, loyalty, and respect for fellow team members. He also wanted to instill in them passion, learning the lessons of both winning and losing, not giving up during tough times, respecting rivals, and – most important of all – gaining self-satisfaction at doing your best at all times. His goal evolved to teaching each girl the importance of always doing their best and applying the lessons learnt from their sports team to all aspects of the lives.

Besides the apparent obstacles encountered along the way that any team in a sporting or business environment would face, the biggest obstacle Allan encountered over the years was that of keeping his communication with his team relevant and current.

When Allan first started as a coach, he was 19-years-old. As a 63-year-old coach, much has changed regarding how the teenage girls in the team view the world: their upbringing, the emergence of social media (and its challenges both positive and negative), all bringing about different team dynamics today compared to those 44 years previous.

So his most significant problem was to keep up with numerous changes and to ensure the communication, motivation and message he wanted to convey as a coach remained relevant and inspirational to each member of his team.

Over 44 years, Allan has been the coach of the most successful team in the world. At the time of writing this book, St Dominic's competition win record is 75%. That's countless wins over 44 years. Their record of finishing on the top three podium positions at all competitions entered is 98.6%! In all that time, Allan innovated team displays, used new methods with his teams, and took teams overseas to compete in world championship competitions. Allan has been motivated to continue year after year, not by the winning of medals and trophies but by seeing the considerable success achieved by the past members of his teams.

The success of St Dominic's goes way beyond what Allan initially expected, and he did achieve his goal of turning a new team into the best of its kind in the world.

Allan says that the biggest lesson he learnt was to never underestimate the resolve and ability of young people who are motivated to strive to do their best in any given situation.

He wrote to me and said:

'I frequently hear that the youth of today are lazy, or spoiled by social media influences, or carry with them a sense of entitlement that they do not think they have to work for. In my experience, it is the adults who are at fault. I have found that as soon as you respect them, give due credit to their ideas and thoughts, show interest in them and give your time to them, they will perform way beyond your wildest expectations. Believe in your team, communicate effectively with them, share your passion with them, show them you care and they will, in turn, believe in you, and no task will then be too big for your team to conquer.'

Comfort zones and why it's hard to leave them

At this stage of the Mindset Fitness Workout program, you've likely achieved your goal, and you're in a warm comfort zone. You will have normalised the challenge, and the changes in your life and things are getting more natural and more routine. Now is the time to set new goals and take on new challenges.

Robin Sharma, author of *The 5am Club*, and motivational and leadership expert reminds us to create big dreams to work towards. He tells us that people need to be laughing at our dreams, or our dreams aren't big enough (robinsharma.com, 2019).

Similarly, author of the bestselling book *The Magic of Big Thinking*, David J Schwartz, writes about the ability of our beliefs to help us pursue bigger goals than we had before. He says, 'Those who believe they can move mountains, do. Those who believe they can't, cannot. Belief triggers the power to do.' He had this idea in 1965, yet so many still struggle to push themselves a little further (Karp, 2014).

Again, it's the ability to dream and believe in big things that motivates us to move forward. Allan's desire to become the coach of the best drum majorette team in the world reminds me that dreaming big can indeed propel you forward.

Familiarity feels safe, it also keeps you stagnant or even stuck in a situation. Many people would feel content to cruise through life, impervious to their potential. They're happy to avoid risks just in case trying would eventuate in a life they didn't hope for. I've coached a few clients who refused to risk trying something new, just in case they failed. Their fear of failure was more significant than their fear of doing nothing. They couldn't handle the thought of their self-esteem taking a hit, and being perceived as a failure. Yet failure and self-worth are not linked. I always explain that you're not a failure when your goals fail to materialise the way you want. An unsuccessful attempt may well be drawing you closer to success each time. And success may not be what you initially imagined.

Before I started running marathons, I would laugh at anyone suggesting that I even go to the gym. However, one serendipitous year, my work colleagues entered a team 12 km fun run/walk. They talked me into joining the team to walk the 12 km to raise money for charity. So I set the goal to get fit enough to walk the distance without getting sore. I started walking longer distances when I took my dog for a walk and slowly became fitter. As the day drew nearer, members of our team started dropping out, until I was the last one attending the race.

I could have quit too, but with 2 weeks to go, I decided to run the 12 km. I never told anyone, I just thought that I might as well get it over with a bit faster since I was going it alone. To everyone's surprise, especially mine, I ran the full 12 km and began a new love and passion for a sport I never dreamed I would ever have. At the time of this writing, I've now completed five full marathons at 42.2 km, and am planning my participation in an 80 km trail race. My goal to walk 12 km with a team didn't materialise. But a new form of success came my way that year, and I'm eternally grateful that I didn't quit.

If you want to step outside your comfort zone, you must extend your boundaries, and you must get out of your usual routine. Think of someone you look up to. Perhaps a mentor or someone in your field who has mastered their art. That successful person would have pushed past their comfort zone to reach their current level of mastery. Again, Allan, in the example above, perfectly demonstrates this characteristic. He took risks, had to learn new skills, and blazed new paths in a sport he'd previously little experience with.

Extending your boundaries and getting out of your routine takes a fair amount of work. It's easy to get comfortable with the familiar and our routines. We resist change. And then when we get excited over new things, the shine wears off quickly. So how do we do it? What are the benefits?

Your comfort zone is neither good nor bad. It's a natural behavioural state where your attitudes, behaviours and daily activities fit a set pattern and routine that minimises stress and risk. It's a state of mental security and provides you with low anxiety, reduced stress and a sense of happiness.

The idea of comfort zones was born in 1908 when psychologists Robert M Yerkes and John D Dodson developed an experiment that showed that a state of relative comfort created a steady level of performance. They found that to maximise performance, people need a state of relative anxiety. Not full anxiety, but rather a state where

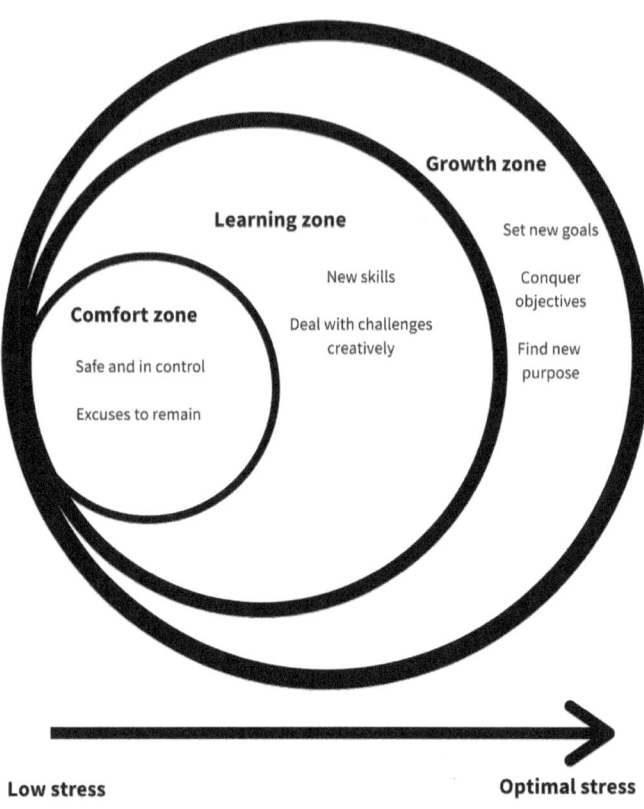

stress levels are only slightly higher than average. They called this 'optimal anxiety', and it's a state of being just outside our comfort zone. The problem is too much anxiety means we become too stressed to perform at all (Yerkes and Dodson, 1908). Since then, the research has been called the Yerkes–Dodson Law, and it's applied to multiple fields (Teigen, 1994).

I'm sure you can relate to this idea of optimal anxiety. If you've ever pushed yourself to accomplish something, you know that when you challenge yourself, you can surprise yourself. Numerous studies support this idea. But pushing too hard can result in less than optimal results, and this can, in turn, reinforce the idea that challenging yourself and going out of your comfort zone is a bad idea. We have a natural tendency to return to a comfortable, relaxed state. Think back to the optimal stress diagram in the previous chapter. This is why it's challenging to get yourself outside of your comfort zone.

Leaving your comfort zone creates increased risk and anxiety, but it should not be demonised as something that holds you back all of the time. It's good to have times where you're not anxious and stressed so that you can reap the benefits when you leave it. A comfort zone can be seen like a frenemy: A friend you rely on, yet who also keeps you reaching a higher potential.

There are other reasons why psychological barriers arise when we're trying to do something new or different. In his book *Reach*, Dr Andy Molinsky describes five obstacles that hold us back:

- **The Authenticity Challenge:** *Feeling that the new behaviour conflicts with your natural style*

- **The Likeability Challenge:** *Worrying that people won't like the latest version of you*

- **The Competence Challenge:** *Feeling that you don't have the skills to 'pull off' whatever you're trying to do*

- **The Resentment Challenge:** *Being annoyed that you need to change your behaviour in the first place*

- **The Morality Challenge:** *Having some concerns about the morality of specific actions or behaviours*

So, with increased anxiety and the psychological barriers we put up to prevent us from trying new things, it's no wonder that many people prefer to stay in the relative safety of their comfort zones.

Leaving your comfort zone

What happens when you leave your comfort zone?

Increased productivity

As mentioned, optimal anxiety is that place where your mental productivity and performance reach their peak. Comfort zones kill productivity because we don't have that sense of unease that we get when we have expectations and deadlines upon us. Comfort zones tend to make us do the minimum required to get by. We lose the drive to learn new things because we don't need to learn anything to help us do things we're comfortable with. We also fall into the 'busy-ness' trap as a way to stay in our comfort zones and avoid doing new things. We feign being busy with lots of activities that aren't challenging at all. Pushing outside your routines and boundaries helps you find smarter ways to work and helps you get more done.

Deal with uncertainty more effectively

When you leave your comfort zone, you also find it easier to deal with new and unexpected changes. Comfort zones make you resistant to change because you don't want anything to disrupt the status quo with uncertainty. Author and research professor Brené Brown explains that one of the worst things we can do is pretend fear and uncertainty don't exist. We do this in our comfort zones. So by taking risks in a controlled fashion and challenging yourself to participate in something new, you can experience uncertainty in a somewhat controlled way.

Push boundaries more easily in the future

When you practise pushing your limits, you'll find it easier to do so in the future. It gets easier over time, and you become used to a state of optimal anxiety. Optimal anxiety can also be described as productive discomfort. As you live in this state more often, it will become more reasonable for you to push further before your performance and productivity wavers. As you challenge yourself, your comfort zone will adjust. What once was a challenging and anxiety-inducing event before will become more comfortable as you repeat it.

Allan speaks about this in his drum majorette story. He says that he rarely feels uncomfortable with new challenges.

The benefits you get from stepping outside your comfort zone can have long-lasting effects outside of productivity and deal with uncertainty. You will undoubtedly experience overall self-improvement from the new skills you'll learn (or from the new country you visit or new food you try or the new job you apply for). I've been involved in many debates where I've been told that the terms 'increased performance' and 'enhanced productivity' sound like 'do more stuff'. This isn't the case. It's about broadening your horizons, experiencing novelty and being more creative.

Some tips to break you out of your comfort zone:

Revisit your greatest accomplishments

All of your past accomplishments were no doubt achieved because you had the courage to step outside your comfort zone. You looked fear in the eye and found out what you were made of. If you find yourself resisting to step outside a comfortable spot, revisit your greatest successes and remember the courage that got you there. Workout 1 in *Flexibility Training* helps you improve at reflecting on successes and failures.

Find the meaning

I've talked a lot about meaning in this book, and it is a game-changer. Stepping out of our comfort zone will be difficult if you don't have a compelling and meaningful reason to push you there. Take the time to visualise why you're doing something so that the idea builds substantial momentum that propels you into inspired action. Workout 1 in *Endurance and Resilience Training* will assist you in finding meaning through knowing your values and vision.

Physically embody the change

Amy Cuddy wrote an excellent book called *Presence: Bringing Your Boldest Self to Your Biggest Challenges*, which she summarises in an excellent Ted Talk. She talks about embodying the mental change we want to see by standing in expansive poses to help increase our sense of power and confidence. While shifts in mindset lead to alterations in the body and emotional state, we can also shift our mental state by posing our bodies in a way that represents the mindset we'd like to have. Try standing in a confident way when you're faced with uncertainty. The more you pose, the more you'll be able to step out of your comfort zone (Cudy, 2018).

Reframe the definition of comfortable

We often think of comfort zones in a way that makes us want to stay there. But that's just one side of the coin. What do you feel when you're in your comfort zone? Perhaps you'd say you feel safe and secure. But could you also mean that you're bored, uninspired, stagnant, or inflexible? Could your comfort zone also be your zone of failure? I challenge you to reframe discomfort to mean growth, learning or purpose and see what happens. Workout 2 in *Flexibility Training* helps you become more natural at finding perspective and reframing.

Take the first step forward

People naturally resist change. It's not the change itself we dislike. Change is perceived as pain in the brain, and we don't like pain! But what if I told you that by taking the smallest step forward tricks your brain into taking action? Mel Robbins discusses a trick in her book called *The 5 Second Rule* where she counts backwards from three and then takes a step towards doing something she would have usually resisted. This forward momentum tricks you into continuing with the next steps after that (Robbins, 2017). The approach boosts confidence since you associate a positive outcome to being outside your comfort zone and motivates you to stick with pursuing it. Workout 1 in *Strength Training* will help you chunk down goals into smaller steps, so you know which action to take first.

Know the worst and best possible outcomes

Have you ever compared the worst and best possible outcomes of a situation? Ask yourself what both of these scenarios look like and then determine the likely outcome. These questions help you identify where your discomfort is coming from and then help you channel your energy towards making the likely case happen. Workout 2 in *Flexibility Training* helps you to identify the worst-case and best-case scenarios.

A word of caution

As alluring as I've made it to push through your comfort zone, there is a risk. You don't want to make it a constant quest. You can't be outside your comfort zone indefinitely. The best results happen when, from time to time, you find yourself in a period of calm and comfort so that you can process your experiences. If you don't, there's a danger that anything new and exciting can quickly become commonplace and boring. This is a phenomenon called hedonistic adaptation, and it occurs when our ability to be impressed by new things becomes ordinary. In one way, being outside our comfort zone drives us forward. But if not managed, it can keep us from appreciating subtleties and the everyday.

Bringing us back to the Mindset Fitness Workout model, it's at this point where you take into account all you've learnt about meaningful goal-setting, willpower and burnout, and habits *before* you step outside your comfort zone. There's a zone of proximal development, and it's there that the magic will continue to happen for you. By building your mindset using the workouts in this book, you keep your brain in peak condition and build the tools within yourself to deal with anything that life throws at you. We're not machines with infinite work capacity, so these workouts are designed to help you avoid burnout.

The aim is to get into a state of optimal anxiety in a controlled way and not to get stressed. Take time to complete the workouts and reflect on your experiences so you can apply lessons to your day to day activities. Once you've mastered that, do something new and exciting. Form new habits. Similarly, don't think that stepping out of your comfort zone means being involved in significant or vast experiences. It may be that learning to meditate pushes you out of your comfort zone just as much as rock-climbing. The goal isn't to become an adrenaline junkie. The goal is to learn what you're capable of in a meaningful way. That's another reason why it's essential to return to a comfortable state sometimes. Don't forget the inspired, creative, productive and slightly uncomfortable moments when you do.

Bibliography

Brené, B. (2019). Articles by Brené Brown. Retrieved December 12, 2019, from https://brenebrown.com/blog.

Cudy, A. (2018). *Presence: Bringing Your Boldest Self to Your Biggest Challenges.* New York: Little, Brown and Company.

Molinksy, A. (2017). *Reach.* USA: Penguin Random House.

Sharma, R. (2019). Do Your Dream? Retrieved December 12, 2019, from https://www.robinsharma.com/article/do-your-dream.

Robbins, M. (2017). *The 5 Second Rule.* USA: Savio Republic.

Schwartz, D. (1965). *The Magic of Thinking Big.* New York: Simon & Schuster.

Yerkes, R. M. & Dodson, J. D. (1908). The relationship of strength of stimulus to rapidity of habit formation. *Journal of Comparative Neurology and Psychology*, 18, pp. 459–482. Retrieved from https://onlinelibrary.wiley.com/doi/abs/10.1002/cne.920180503.

Teigen, K. (1994). Yerkes-Dodson: A Law for all Seasons. *Theory & Psychology*, 4(4), pp. 525–547. Retrieved https://journals.sagepub.com/doi/abs/10.1177/0959354394044004.

Part 2

The Mindset Fitness Workouts

Now that you know the steps in the model, it's time to introduce you to the areas in which you will improve your fitness. Part 2 of this book describes each mindset area and the related workouts designed to assist you.

The diagram below shows workouts in each mindset area that you can select when you're in need.

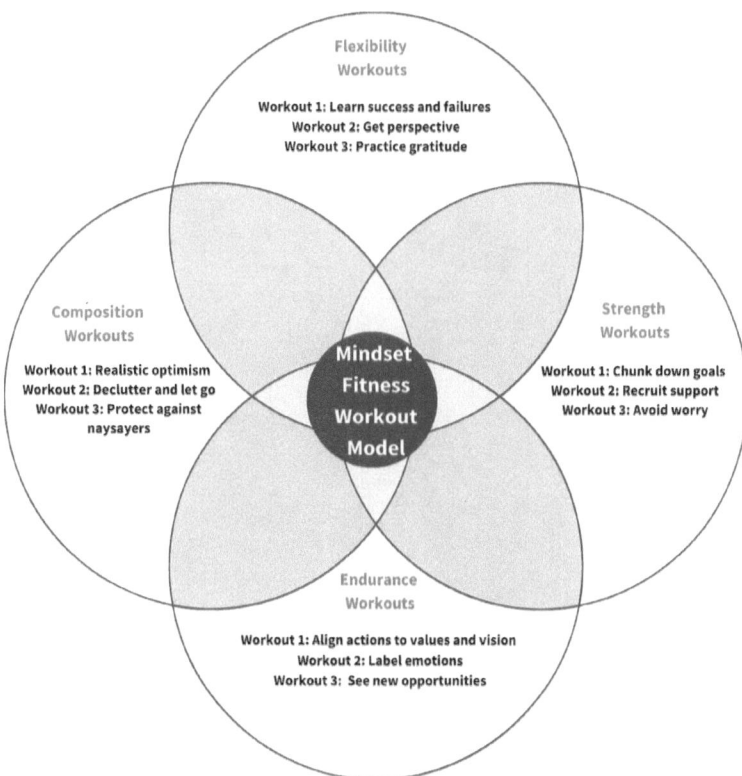

5
Flexibility Training

'Remain firm about your goals, but flexible about your methods.'

Managing Interpersonal Conflict (1992) by
William A Donohue

The challenge many face today is that they know how to make plans, but they don't know how to react when something changes or when an unplanned event occurs. They can't respond adequately to an unforeseen situation. There often comes a point in the pursuit of your goals where you realise your plan may not be the right way to go anymore.

Alex Gamble is a personal trainer and coach and the founder and owner of an online personal training academy and mobile app. His goal is a big one! He wants to help as many people as he can to get into the best shape of their lives. Whether that means physically – being fitter, stronger, healthier – or through being mentally stronger and healthier. In the early stages of Alex starting his coaching business, he realised that if people were to achieve this, they would begin to love themselves a lot more. Contributing to that happiness gives Alex an immense sense of satisfaction and joy. He also has an internal drive to be the best person he can be and to make his family and himself proud of his accomplishments. He refuses to be the type of person to reach old age and think 'I could have done more.'

Alex has never put an exact number on the amount of people he wants to help.

He knows that there are billions of people in this world, and each year people are getting more overweight, more unhappy and slightly less fit. The more people Alex could help, the more he can reverse those trends. So he developed a plan to become a personal trainer.

After a few short years, Alex realised there was a limit to the number of people or clients he could help one-on-one every week. His goal was still the same, but he needed to adjust his methods. This was the beginning of his idea to create an online academy. The academy would give anyone from anywhere in the world access to video content about workouts, workout techniques, fitness plans and nutrition.

His biggest obstacle was learning how to put himself out there to achieve this fully. If he were indeed to help hundreds, thousands and maybe even millions of people, he would have to think a lot bigger. To promote the academy, Alex first had to get comfortable with sharing content about himself and promoting himself over social media. He not only had to be okay with it, but he also had to excel at it and love it!

To create an online presence and video platform for thousands to access, Alex needed to feel comfortable in front of the camera. At the same time, he needed to invest all his energy into looking after all his current clients while building his brand. He also needed to spend most of his savings into the business with no guarantee it would work and with no promise of making that money back. That's a significant risk that many wouldn't be willing to take. Alex saw it as an opportunity to learn about himself and learn about the direction he wanted his life to take.

Alex wasn't immune from doubt, although he says the moments of doubt were short-lived and didn't happen often. He says that doubts enter everyone's mind, and the key for him was not to avoid it but instead know how to shift his mindset rapidly. Alex personally counters his doubts with tremendous self-belief and internal positive self-talk. He reminds himself that quitting is not an option and that he only really fails if he gives up. He then moves onto a more helpful mindset to keep moving forward. He refuses to get to the end of a road without 'even giving it a proper crack!' One thing that has always helped him avoid self-doubt is being confident in his craft, his knowledge, and what he does for a living. He's constantly learning!

Alex practises gratitude daily by merely thinking about how lucky he is to live this life and have the opportunities he does. Most of the time, his gratitude comes to him in the purest forms, and he believes it's the simple things that most people forget. He reminds himself daily of how lucky he is to have fresh food on the table, a roof over his head and running water. He says he always tries to make a conscious effort to be kind to everyone and be grateful for anything they do for him, big or small. He also loves to travel to developing countries a few times each year, since he loves seeing and experiencing their cultures. This always makes him extraordinarily grateful and happy with his life. He actively encourages people with a negative view of their lives to visit those places. Seeing happy people, despite working 16-hour days, 7 days a week for below minimum wage is a humbling experience.

Alex has learnt many lessons in the pursuit of his goals. He says that to progress and succeed, he's needed to stay open-minded with a 'white belt mentality'. He describes this as 'Always learning and being adaptable with my goals. I'm willing to go all-in, and believe that I will succeed no matter how many times I must change the path or route to my goal.'

He also says that everyone needs to acknowledge small and big wins along the way.

Alex says it's easy to smash a goal and not even notice because you already have sights set on the next one. Another important lesson he shared was that when you're pursuing a goal, you must 110% believe in yourself no matter what people tell you. He says that many people will try to bring you down to their level or tell you that you're crazy or that you're ridiculous, but that's because they can't see what you can see. This is often the people closest to you, which makes it particularly tricky. Alex has had family and friends try to hold him back, even though they might have done it out of love because they didn't want to see him hurt or fail. In this instance, he says the most important thing is to back yourself and keep believing in yourself because that's all you need.

While Alex says he hasn't achieved his goal (yet), he's ticked off dozens of small goals along the way. Alex has helped hundreds of people, and he has followers on social media into the thousands. He's proud of what he's achieved but, in his mind, he has a lot more to give. It's just the beginning for Alex!

Flexibility is key

When we look at Alex's story and his goals, we can see that he realised that to achieve what he wanted to do, he had to change his method of delivery. He saw that there might be a more efficient way for him to achieve his goal. Too often, people consider letting go of their dreams or goals when things don't go according to plan or when they come across a problem. Everyone comes across this sort of obstacle at some point or another.

Research suggests that good problem-solvers are qualitatively different from poor problem-solvers. Good problem-solvers are flexible and resourceful and create new ways to think through problems. They have alternative approaches if they get stuck. This create ways of making progress when they hit roadblocks. They also have a certain kind of disposition and a willingness to pit themselves against difficult challenges under the assumption that they'll be able to make progress on them, and the tenacity to keep at the task when others have given up (Schoenfeld, 2007).

People who can plot out new routes are the ones who reach the destination. When a non-flexible person is thrown a curveball, they get flustered, complain about it or even give up.

What does being flexible mean?

The word flexible is defined as 'the capability to bend easily without breaking'. Someone with a flexible mind can overcome challenges and embrace change. They find the path of least resistance. Everyone knows that flexibility is the opposite of being rigid. It means not being set in your ways and being open to new ideas and new ways of thinking.

According to work done by Steve Zaccaro (1991), there are three types of flexibility:

1. **Cognitive flexibility:** *The ability to use different thinking strategies and mental frameworks*

2. **Emotional flexibility:** *The ability to vary one's approach to dealing with emotions and the emotions of others*

3. **Dispositional flexibility:** *The ability to remain optimistic and realistic*

By learning and practising behaviours that boost your cognitive, emotional, and dispositional flexibility, you can become more adaptable.

If you have a flexible mindset, then you do not fear change. You understand that you can manipulate an unexpected situation and leverage it to your advantage. Tony Robbins, author and motivational speaker, often says, 'Stay committed to your decisions but flexible in your approach.' (Robbins, 2012).

Why is being flexible important?

Flexibility is a critical skill in an ever-changing, fast-paced world. If one strategy fails, you must be ready to try another. Business leaders must adopt a flexible mindset to cater to the changing needs of their customers. Parents must be flexible in managing their schedules to provide for their family's needs.

A 2014 study found that psychological flexibility is negatively associated with emotional exhaustion and positively associated with performance. Also, psychological flexibility is found to attenuate the negative effects of emotional job demands on emotional exhaustion and performance. The results support the importance of personal resources, like psychological flexibility, in buffering the negative effects of emotional job demands on emotional exhaustion and performance (Onwezen, Veldhoven, & Biron, 2014). When you demonstrate flexibility, your colleagues, friends, and family know that they can count on you during times of uncertainty or change. If you're flexible, you will likely be more involved in a variety of projects and teams. This provides you with more variety, and there will be less conflict and more understanding in all your relationships.

Flexibility can be seen as the key to success for a multitude of reasons. Perhaps the most important is that flexibility helps you overcome challenges. It can open your world to opportunities that you never thought you would have a chance to experience. I relate being flexible in the mind to being flexible in the muscles. Flexible muscles give you a better range of movement and mobility.

By training your brain to be more flexible, you increase your versatility in your goal-setting and start to develop an abundance mentality.

This abundance mentality – where we know that there's enough out there for us – negates feelings of helplessness, hopelessness, and loss of motivation that can lead to burnout. Alex demonstrates an abundance mentality, with his thoughts of being able to achieve whatever he sets his mind to and having enough motivation inside him to make it happen.

I believe that being flexible has the following benefits:

Less pain, more gain

In the same way that your body feels better when your muscles are flexible, opening your mind to new possibilities creates fewer aches and pains. Being rigid in your goal pursuit can sometimes mean blindly doing tasks that aren't going to get you any closer to achieving what you want. How tedious and painful is that? Having mental flexibility means every obstacle is viewed as an opportunity for learning. This gives you a confident and calm demeanour when solving problems. And the more focused you are, the higher the chance of the issues getting resolved and less long-term pain.

Balance

When you increase muscular flexibility, your posture and balance are likely to improve. Flexible thinking also lets you achieve balance in your lifestyle. You can adapt goals to how you're feeling, to life experiences that pop up, and to new opportunities. So instead of working yourself too hard in the rigid pursuit of one thing, you achieve more balance in your life. You can attend important family events that you would otherwise miss. You can change your schedule. You have more control over your time, and you can better understand when you'll accomplish more.

A positive state of mind

The physical benefits of stretching and flexibility can extend to a relaxed state of mind. Flexible thinking also helps you feel calm, relaxed and less under pressure. People with flexible mindsets have a unique ability to perceive emotions and feelings. Contrary to a fixed mindset that's shallow and insecure – those with flexible mindsets can treat everyone fairly, even under challenging circumstances. This increases the wellbeing and positive emotions of people around them.

Improved performance

Anyone with flexible muscles has a better range of motion and performs better in sport or other physical pursuits. The same applies to flexible thinking. You can enhance your performance through the ability to overcome challenges.

The case for rigid goal-setting

Various sources estimate that an adult makes about 35,000 decisions each day (Sahakian & Labuzetta, 2013). We live in an information-overloaded, decision-fatigued world. You only have to look at the choices in mayonnaise brands on the grocery store shelf to prove this point. In the book *Paradox of Choice – Why More Is Less*, psychologist Barry Schwartz discusses how people benefit from the need to make fewer decisions. A rigid approach to goal pursuit offers just that by setting predetermined steps for achieving a goal and eliminating or reducing the number of unnecessary 'decision points' that arise. Theoretically, the goal becomes more likely to be achieved and potentially feels easier to accomplish (Schwartz, 2016).

So what's best?

When it comes to people's behaviour, it's context that matters. In situations where the goal is relatively simple, and the motivation to achieve that goal is quite strong, taking a flexible approach typically works best. In situations where the change required is complex, or if motivation levels are low, a rigid or combination approach could be more effective.

What undermines flexibility?

The following habits and characteristics will undermine flexibility:

- *A failure to maintain perspective on situations and narrowing your focus to thoughts that may not be facts*
- *Seeing only the negative in a situation or creating barriers to success*
- *Not experiencing gratitude*

Do you recognise any of these traits in yourself? If yes, consider one or more of the workouts in the following pages.

Bibliography

Burns, D. (2000). *Feeling Good.* New York: HarperCollins.

Nisbett, R. (2007). *Thought and Feeling: Cognitive Alteration of Feeling States.* USA: Transaction Publishers.

Onwezen, M. C., Veldhoven, M. V. & Biron, M. (2014). The role of psychological flexibility in the demands–exhaustion–performance relationship. *European Journal of Work and Organizational Psychology,* 23(2), pp. 163–176. Retrieved from https://tandfonline.com/doi/full/10.1080/1359432x.2012.742242.

Robbins, T. (2012). *Awaken The Giant Within.* New York: Free Press.

Sahakian, B. & LaBuzetta, J. (2013). *Bad Moves: How Decision Making Goes Wrong, and the Ethiocs of Smart Drugs.* Oxford: Oxford University Press.

Schoenfeld, A. (2007) *Assessing Mathematical Proficiency.* New York: Cambridge University Press.

Schwartz, B. (2016). *The Paradox of Choice: Why More Is Less: How the Culture of Abundance Robs Us of Satisfaction.* New York: Ecco Press.

Zaccaro, S.J., Gilbert, J.A., Thor, K.K, & Mumford, M.D. (1991). Leadership and social intelligence: Linking social perceptiveness and behavioral flexibility to leader effectiveness. *Leadership Quarterly,* 2, pp. 317–331. Retrieved from https://www.sciencedirect.com/science/article/pii/104898439190018W.

Workouts for Flexibility

Workout 1: Learn from the day's successes and failures

What is the workout?

This workout is about the art of reflection. It's reflective practice in its purest form and thinking about what you do and have done. It's similar to learning from experience, in that you think about what happened, how you responded, and decide what you would do differently next time.

Reflection is a great way to increase confidence and become more proactive. It teaches you that you're in control of your choices and actions. If something went wrong, it will help you decide how you could respond more constructively next time and whether you can prevent it from happening again. Similarly, when something goes well, the workout allows you to celebrate and learn how to repeat success. This workout creates a way of studying your own experiences to improve the way you work and move through your goal. It's handy for helping you to continue learning throughout your life. Remember that it's not enough to only reflect on what happened, you must create a clear action plan for what you will do next to make reflective practice meaningful.

How does this workout improve flexibility?

Learning from success and failure allows you to set new goals and actions and improve your plan. If everything is viewed as an opportunity to learn, you're more likely to overcome obstacles.

When should you consider doing this workout?

If you struggle to understand why things happened the way they did or if you're getting stressed over things you can't control, this workout will help you find some meaning.

Instructions

Step 1: Find a suitable method

The only goal of self-reflection is to look inward on situations and being present to the thoughts that arise. Walking, running, sitting in a chair, or writing is an excellent way to practise self-reflection, and there's no rule as to where you should do this. Find a current habit to which you would like to attach this workout.

Step 2: Schedule time

Setting time specifically for self-reflection helps you hold yourself accountable for practising this essential skill. I suggest starting small with 10 minutes each time. As you hone your self-reflection skills, you'll be able to reflect for extended periods. The workout requires a commitment to be effective. If you choose the morning, reflect on your experiences from the previous day. If you select the evening, reflect on your experiences of that day.

Step 3: What happened today?

Ask yourself the following questions about the day:
- *What happened during the day?*
- *What problem did I encounter today?*
- *What successes did I experience?*
- *What was my role in that problem, and in my success?*
- *What were the consequences?*

Step 4: So what does this mean?

Ask yourself the following questions about the meaning of success/failure:

- *What was going through my mind during the problem?*
- *What should I have done to prevent the problem?*
- *What did I do to contribute to the success?*

Step 5: Now what do I do?

Ask yourself the following questions about what you might do next:

- *What do I need to do next time?*
- *What can I do to repeat my success?*

Workout 2: Get perspective

What is the workout?

To understand this workout, you must first understand how some people become trapped by their patterns of negative thinking, and become lost in their thoughts. Psychiatrist Dr Aaron T Beck laid the groundwork for much of what we now know about cognitive distortions and found that we interpret our experiences through arbitrary judgement, over-generalisation and distortion (Nisbett, 2007). The more someone tries to 'think' their way out of a situation, the more they become entangled in those negative thoughts, until everything starts to look bleak and miserable. I call these types of thinking 'pits of despair'. Positive psychology more accurately refers to them as thinking traps. In his book *Feeling Good: The New Mood Therapy*, Dr David Burns outlines common cognitive distortions that form the basis for irrational thinking. The diagram taken from his book shows how this happens.

Through the combination of Beck's and Burns' work and the work of other positive psychologists like Dr Martin Seligman, we can see five common thinking traps, namely mindreading, 'it's all about me', 'it's all their fault', catastrophising, and helplessness.

Mindreading

Mindreading occurs when you believe you already know what another person is thinking. It's one of the most common and potentially damaging thinking traps to fall into. This is caused by prejudging a situation and believing that we know how another person is going to react. This results in getting caught in negative spirals of thoughts without giving the other a person an opportunity to respond for themselves. Some people can spend hours imagining all the things someone thinks or will say. They imagine how arguments will occur and how terrible they're going to feel afterwards. They convince themselves that they know exactly how someone is going to respond.

It's all about me

This thinking trap revolves around your mistaken belief that you are, in fact, the centre of the universe. Sometimes people become wrapped up in themselves and assume that everything's about them, even though it's not. They become consumed with their part in the situation. The worry about how it will impact them, what the negative consequences will be for them, and how much they're to blame. By falling into the trap of 'me', people forget that there are other people involved and that those people may even be suffering more than them. The antidote is the ability to step back and look at it from a broader, less self-centred perspective.

It's all their fault

Typically the opposite of the 'me' trap, is the 'it's them' trap. This places the blame on everyone else. Many find it easy to place blame on others, especially when they're angry or hurt. This leads to bitterness, resentment, and frustration. By placing the blame on others, people lose the ability to see how they might resolve the issues themselves. Seligman's work on learned optimism explains how the ability to correctly identify your share of responsibility for situations is critical for shifting towards a more optimistic mindset.

Catastrophising

Do you always find yourself worrying about the worst-case scenario? Do you have thoughts about being fired for making a mistake? Or do you become concerned about your partner leaving you for arguing about a T-shirt on the floor? This is called catastrophising, and it occurs when negative thoughts run away and lead to certain doom. Smalls problems become more and more pronounced as someone imagines increasingly devastating possibilities and ends to a problem. This leaves them stressed and overwhelmed.

Helplessness

The final trap is helplessness. The feeling of helplessness is a conditioned response in people who've had repeated exposure to situations and circumstances over which they had no control. The more they experience an inability to affect their surroundings positively, the more they develop the belief that they are helpless. Eventually, they give up trying, believing that there isn't any action they can take to make a difference.

Because we get attached to the perspectives that we hold, it can be difficult to change them. We can feel convicted in the views we hold and many of these 'lenses' in which we see life are subconscious, and inbred into our thinking. We have loyalty and even 'rightness' about the perspectives we hold. Seligman's work shows that consciously disputing your thoughts with fact-based alternatives can help shift you closer to optimism and action.

This workout teaches you how to get some new perspectives on your problems. It helps you avoid blowing issues out of proportion in your mind. It prevents catastrophic thinking, blaming yourself, and jumping to conclusions, which all undermine flexibility and mindset. This workout allows you to stay in perspective by conducting reality testing against such thoughts.

How does this workout improve flexibility?

By being more realistic in our thinking, we don't only see one way to do things. If you can see five ways to do something, you can pick which way you like best, make space for others to do it differently or enjoy a variety of approaches to reach your goals.

When should you consider doing this workout?

If you recognise any of the mind traps discussed, a new perspective will help you shift your thinking.

Instructions

Step 1: Find a quiet place

Choose a specific time in the day to find a quiet place. Sit down and journal about the event that's triggered a thinking trap.

Step 2: Describe the situation

Write down the facts about the challenging situation and avoid writing down emotions.

Step 3: Describe different scenarios

Write down the worst case scenario of what will happen as a result of the situation. Then the best case. Then the probable case.

Step 4: Review the thinking traps

Consider any thinking traps you've let yourself fall into. Do any of your cases have any irrational thoughts or beliefs about the situation?

Step 5: Reframe

Reframe the thought and write down one action that will get you closer to the probable case.

Workout 3: Practise gratitude

What is the workout?

In my discussions with Alex, he often mentioned his gratitude for his life and actively put himself in situations where he felt thankful for his opportunities and blessings. In his book *Thanks! How the New Science of Gratitude Can Make You Happier*, Dr Robert Emmons shows that practising gratitude can increase your happiness levels by about 25%. This workout is about bringing more appreciation into your life. The more you practise feeling and expressing gratitude, the more the feeling will come to you spontaneously in the future.

How does this workout improve flexibility?

People become frustrated when too they're controlling and inflexible. They want the world to live by their rules and see only the negative in situations around them while failing to see the world through gratitude and opportunity. Taking the time to be thankful has many benefits for wellbeing and happiness. It creates more optimism, decreases anxiety and depression, and improves goal attainment. There's also evidence that gratitude is associated with fewer symptoms of illness.

When should you consider doing this workout?

If you find yourself struggling to be optimistic, losing hope, or losing motivation, gratitude will move you towards a better mindset. This also may be helpful when you feel anxious or upset about a situation or event.

Instructions

Step 1: Decide when to practise

Find a time to practise, whether in the morning or evening, practise this workout during your shower or bath ritual.

Step 2: Find five

While in the shower, make a conscious effort to find five things you were grateful for in that day or the day before. Sometimes it may be as simple as being thankful for hot water, a cup of coffee and sleep. Other times you may feel grateful for family. The key is to find five things you genuinely feel gratitude for.

6

Strength Training

*'The secret of life is this: When you hear the sound of
the cannons, walk toward them.'*

Marcel France

Everyone knows that to achieve greatness, you must work hard, engage in learning, push through painful experiences, and maintain rigorous effort. This requires strength.

Michelle Jenkins is the CEO for a large community organisation based in Western Australia. She's had an inspiring career in the finance sector and the community services sector and led multiple teams and organisations. Michelle sets two significant goals every year. One is a professional goal that's about what she wants to achieve in her current role or for her career. The second is a personal goal, which varies each year. One year, Michelle wanted to learn to drive a truck. Another year, she wanted to improve her Spanish speaking skills.

To date, she says that the goal that was most meaningful professionally was when she undertook a master's degree in business leadership. She wanted a degree that she knew she would use, and which would advance her opportunities and give her a reason to focus on her leadership skills. Michelle did this while working full time and with a young child still in school. She says that it wasn't easy. Even so, she obtained her degree in 2010.

She set her most meaningful personal goal around the same time as starting her degree. Michelle found herself getting divorced with only $10,000 in her bank account, with two dogs and a 10-year-old. It meant re-homing her dogs so someone would rent her a house and then dealing with the trauma of the marriage breakdown and the loss of best friends. She set a goal to find her family a permanent home. This was nearly 15 years ago, and for the past 10 years, Michelle has lived in her own home.

To make her goals more manageable, Michelle made a point of reading her course material during the week. She'd then picture in her mind what she wanted to write in her assignments, outlining the case studies and the approach. Every Friday night, Michelle would sit down after work and write something towards completing her assignments. As it got closer to the submission date, she would pull an 'all-nighter'. She would sit and edit everything into a document that was suitable for submission. Michelle then rewarded herself with a week of relaxation and got a massage or similar treat.

Michelle managed to save some money and fell in love with a house near to where she was living at the time. She knew that if she could get the stamp duty together and get a loan, that she could have the house. Michelle never doubted her ability to purchase that house, and 6 weeks later she moved into her new home.

Michelle says that asking for help when you need it is the key to being successful. Many heads are better than one on a problem, so if you can, share the load and ask for help from those whose skills are better suited to the problem. In her professional life, Michelle has always believed in not burning bridges and maintaining healthy and positive relationships. If people are no longer part of her network, it's because they don't add any value to the relationship. Michelle also reads voraciously and attends many courses, all of which give her the skills and toolkits to achieve her goals. Michelle says she'll often call on a close group of mentors and coaches when she needs help with a specific problem. From their confidential feedback, she can make a call on the action she needs to take. She does say, that as a leader, sometimes the support you recruit is your own! You are the one who must make the decision, and some decisions can be hard. She says that in those situations, it's essential not to be hard on yourself because it is often the situation, and not you personally, that's creating the problem.

Michelle still worries from time to time. She says she worries about everything but doesn't always share it with others. Her mindset is that we all worry about things, good and bad, but it's how we deal with those worries that helps us to get through. Michelle meditates to help herself deal with her fears. She has a large gum tree in her garden, and she sits there with a coffee and thinks about things, breathing in the air and just being mindful of her surroundings.

Michelle counts her blessings for her life and what she's achieved, and she asks herself what lessons she's learnt along the way and what she wants to improve in the future. She will look at what she's worried about and asks if she can change it. If she can, she takes stock of her options, decides how to achieve them, and thinks about whom she can ask for help.

Another key to Michelle's success over the years has been that she's very clear about what she wanted and why she wanted it. She says she always could make things happen and knows she can achieve anything she sets her mind to. She's also learnt to break things down into small pieces and complete them one at a time. If she can't visualise it, then she can't get passionate about it because she doesn't know what it looks like. To drive a business to new heights, she must have a plan and then action it and believe it will happen.

Michelle says that along the way you'll have setbacks – and it's essential to ask yourself if you're still on the right goal, or whether you got it wrong. Share your ideas with those you trust to give you sound advice and ask them if they would change anything, then revisit the original plan with that feedback.

All in all, Michelle says that her goals involve an element of planning, which leads to some good fortune. Michelle believes that we create our own luck in this world, and that we can be or do anything we want – but we must want it enough to make it happen.

Being strong-minded – what does it mean?

Looking back on Michelle's story, I see an enormous amount of strength in her ability to sustain energy during challenging times. Being strong-minded means being determined. In the book *Talent*

Is Overrated, Geoffrey Colvin argues that talent is not necessarily a gift bestowed upon the fortunate but something we acquire through deliberate practice. Building a strong mindset also requires deliberate practice (Colvin, 2018). And a strong mindset is crucial for dealing with sudden changes in our work, relationships or lives. Michelle's life took unexpected twists and turns, yet she faced each one courageously.

In Michelle's story, you can see that she faced setbacks and that she engaged in learning and deliberate practice to continue to pursue her goals.

Depending on who you talk to, or what you read, people define strength in many ways. People often think of mental toughness as grit and resilience, and these ideas share characteristics that individuals will generally term as mental strength or mental toughness. Mental toughness has its highest profile in sport, but its impact is now recognised in a wide range of other domains. It's an umbrella term that entails positive psychological resources, which are important across a range of achievement contexts (Clough et al., 2002; Crust and Clough, 2011; Gucciardi et al., 2015a).

Indeed, the ability to sustain self-belief, remain passionate and goal-oriented, and the ability to withstand stressors and adversity are all aspects of 'tough' behaviour (Van Haitsma et al., 2019). Increased mental toughness has been associated with faster running times from cross-country runners (Mahoney et al., 2014) and better performance in soldiers (Adler et al., 2015).

If we think of mental strength as a concept, we can think of popular heroes. Heroes like Robin Hood and James Bond embody the characteristics that we've valued throughout the ages. I respect other types of heroes, such as Kenyan marathon runner Eliud Kipchoge, who in the month of me writing this chapter, became the first man to run a sub-2-hour marathon. His mental strength to achieve this is nothing short of deserving the title *heroic*. He trained for this fantastic feat for 5 years and failed his first attempt. Heroes show us what it's like to have the mental toughness to achieve great things. They create worlds full of possibilities.

But what does mental strength look like to you and me in normal situations? My definition of what it means to have a strong mind is to have the capacity, mental skill, and resources to face all types of challenges. A strong mind gives you the energy and stamina to face a problem while still allowing you to know when to quit, and when to keep going.

Some say mental strength is a mindset comprised of several qualities and attitudes. Clough et al. (2002) described mentally tough individuals as 'tending to be sociable and outgoing as they can remain calm and relaxed. They are competitive in many situations and have lower anxiety levels than others. With a high sense of self-belief and an unshakable faith that they control their destiny, these individuals can remain relatively unaffected by competition or adversity.'

I've chosen to condense the qualities described in numerous studies that I think are relevant for the workouts in this book. Think of your hero for a moment, or look at Michelle's story, and see if you recognise any of these qualities that follow here:

Confidence

Confidence is a personal belief about your ability to meet your goals.

Courage

Courage is the ability to see obstacles as challenges to be met head-on rather than threats to be avoided.

Commitment

People are unsuccessful when they lack commitment. Commitment is not an inherent trait. Commitment is the result of working hard and concentrating on bringing about the desired result. No-one succeeds overnight. Nobody fails overnight either. A fully committed person can find a creative solution to almost any task.

Control

Control is having the certainty that you can shape your destiny rather than passively accepting events as they come along.

Purpose

A purpose that's in alignment with your values creates a strong sense of dedication. Strong-minded people express these attitudes and skills daily.

Mental toughness shares similarities with resilience in that both concepts promote positive adaptation in the face of adversity. I go into more detail about resilience in later chapters, but mental strength is distinct from resilience in two important ways.

First, resilience encompasses a range of protective processes, such as creating a social network, and is not directly measured, but rather indirectly inferred (Luthar et al., 2006). Mental strength, on the other hand, is a measurable and specific set of traits. Second, the concept of resilience presupposes the existence of risk in the environment, but mental strength does not. Mental toughness not only relates to an individual's reactions to risk and stress but also entails a proactive tendency to seek out challenges for personal growth (Gucciardi, 2017).

Why is a strong mindset necessary?

Numerous studies show that there's an apparent link between mental strength and performance. Whether it's in the workplace, at school or university, or with sport, mental strength allows people to perform better. It also aids people in being more efficient and more conscientious of the work they're doing.

People with good mental strength are also far more likely to demonstrate various positive psychological traits, more efficient coping strategies and positive outcomes in education and mental health (Lin et al., 2017). Michelle's example shows her positive outlook, even through challenges.

She did not walk away from her problems, and confronted challenges positively.

Strong-minded people almost always get to enjoy a greater sense of wellbeing. Mental strength brings several benefits with it, including the following:

- *Better sleep quality – a study by Brand et al. in 2014 showed individuals who scored high on mental toughness displayed higher sleep efficiency, fewer awakenings after sleep onset as well as more deep sleep and REM sleep.*

- *Being more able to handle stress – mentally tough individuals seem to cope more effectively and tend to perform better under pressure (Kaiseler et al., 2009).*

- *Increased mental strength, leading to improved work performance – there's a link between people with mental strength and ambition. Marchant et al. (2009) showed that higher levels of mental toughness were associated with more senior managerial positions.*

- *Improved persistence, effort or perseverance represents a behavioural signature of mental toughness (Gucciardi et al., 2016).*

While some people may naturally be more mentally tough than others, you can develop mental strength over your lifetime. It will not only pay off when dealing with obstacles, but it will also become a habit and part of your identity.

What undermines mental strength?

The following habits and characteristics undermine mental strength:

- *Becoming overwhelmed by large goals that seem impossible to achieve*

- *Failing to recruit support*

- *Engaging in too much paralysing worry and not taking action or steps forward*

Do you recognise any of these traits in yourself? If yes, consider one or more of the workouts in the following pages.

Bibliography

Adler, A.B., Bliese, P.D., Pickering, M.A., Hammermeister, J., Williams, J., Harada, C., Csoka, L., Holliday, B. & Ohlson, C. (2015). Mental skills training with basic combat training soldiers: A group-randomized trial, *Journal Applied Psychology*, 100 (2015), pp. 1752–1764. Retrieved from https://psycnet.apa.org/record/2015-23324-001.

Carbonell, D. (2016). *Worry Trick*. [Place of publication not identified]: New Harbinger Pub.

Cheng, J., Teevan, J., Iqbal, S.T. & Bernstein, M.S. (2015). Break It Down: A Comparison of Macro- and Microtasks, Proceedings of the 33rd Annual ACM Conference on Human Factors in Computing Systems, April 18–23, 2015, Seoul, Republic of Korea. Retrieved from https://dl.acm.org/doi/abs/10.1145/2702123.2702146.

Clough, P., Earle, K. & Sewell, D. (2002). 'Mental toughness: the concept and its measurement'. *Solutions in Sport Psychology*, (pp. 32–43). Boston: Cengage Learning.

Crust, L. & Clough, P. (2011). Developing mental toughness: from research to practice. *Journal of Sport Psychology*, Action 2, pp. 21–32. Retrieved from https://www.tandfonline.com/doi/abs/10.1080/21520704.2011.563436.

Colvin, G. (2018). Ta*lent Is Overrated: What Really Separates World-Class Performers from Everybody Else*. New York: Portfolio/Penguin.

Feeney, B. & Collins, N. (2014). A New Look at Social Support: A Theoretical Perspective on Thriving Through Relationships. *Personality and Social Psychology Review*, 19(2), pp. 113–147. Retrieved from https://journals.sagepub.com/doi/abs/10.1177/1088868314544222.

Gratias, M. (2020). Melissa Gratias, PhD. *Productivity Specialist*. Retrieved January 28, 2020, from https://melissagratias.com.

Gu, J., Strauss, C., Bond, R. & Cavanagh, K. (2015). How do mindfulness-based cognitive therapy and mindfulness-based stress reduction improve mental health and wellbeing? A systematic review and meta-analysis of mediation studies. *Clinical Psychology Review*, 37(37), pp. 1–12. Retrieved from https://sciencedirect.com/science/article/pii/s0272735815000197.

Kaiseler, M., Polman, R. & Nicholls, A. (2009). Mental toughness, stress, stress appraisal, coping and coping effectiveness in sport. *Personality and Individual Differences*, 47, pp. 728–733. Retrieved from https://www.sciencedirect.com/science/article/abs/pii/S0191886909002748.

Latham, G.P. & Locke, E.A. (2015). The Science and Practice of Goal Setting in Wiley Encyclopedia of Management (eds C.L. Cooper, D.E. Guest and D.J. Needle). doi:10.1002/9781118785317.weom050031.

Luthar, S. S., Sawyer, J. A. & Brown, P. J. (2006). Conceptual issues in studies of resilience. Annals of the New York Academy of Sciences, 1094, pp. 105–115. Retrieved from https://nyaspubs.onlinelibrary.wiley.com/doi/abs/10.1196/annals.1376.009.

Mahoney, J. W., Gucciardi, D. F., Ntoumanis, N. & Mallet, C. J. (2014). Mental toughness in sport: motivational antecedents and associations with performance and psychological healt*h*. *Journal Sport Exercise Psychology*, 36, pp. 281–292. Retrieved from https://journals.humankinetics.com/view/journals/jsep/36/3/article-p281.xml.

Marchant, D. C., Polman, R. C. J., Clough, P., Jackson, J. G., Levy, A. R. & Nicholls, A. R. (2009). Mental toughness: managerial and age differences. *Journal of Managerial Psychology*, 24, pp. 428–437. Retrieved from https://www.emerald.com/insight/content/doi/10.1108/02683940910959753/full/html.

Gucciardi, D. F. (2017). Mental toughness: progress and prospects. *Current Opinion in Psychology*, 16, pp. 17–23. Retrieved from https://www.sciencedirect.com/science/article/pii/S2352250X16301440.

Gucciardi, D. F., Hanton, S., Gordon, S., Mallett, C. J. & Temby, P. (2015a). The concept of mental toughness: tests of dimensionality, nomological network, and traitness. *Journal of Personality*, 83, pp. 26–44. Retrieved from https://onlinelibrary.wiley.com/doi/abs/10.1111/jopy.12079.

Gucciardi, D., Peeling, P., Ducker, K. & Dawson, B. (2016). When the going gets tough: Mental toughness and its relationship with behavioural perseverance. *Journal of Science and Medicine in Sport*, 19(1), pp. 81–86. Retrieved from https://www.sciencedirect.com/science/article/abs/pii/S144024401400632X.

Van Haitsma, T.A., Gonzalez, S.P., Swider, N.S., De Laura, A.C., Costa, D., Salinas, T. & Mc Gough, S. (2019). An Examination of Short-Term Mental Conditioning or Mindfulness Training on Physiological, Psychological, and Performance Outcomes during a Cycling Task, *International Journal of Sports Science* (2019), 9(2), pp. 35–46. Retrieved from http://article.sapub.org/10.5923.j.sports.20190902.03.html.

Lin, Y., Mutz, J., Clough, P. & Papageorgiou, K. (2017). Mental Toughness and Individual Differences in Learning, Educational and Work Performance, Psychological Well-being, and Personality: A Systematic Review. *Frontiers in Psychology*. 8. Retrieved from https://www.frontiersin.org/articles/10.3389/fpsyg.2017.01345/full.

Workouts for Strength

Workout 1: Chunk down goals

What is the workout?

Having ambitious goals to aim for is positive. But spending too much time contemplating the vast distance between where you are now and where you want to be can be demotivating. Ambitious goals can be intimidating and demoralising when they're finished inspiring you. The secret is to break your goal down into lots of smaller steps that will gradually move you towards where you want to be. I like the term 'chunking down' for this. It involves creating actionable short-term goals and then taking one action to move you towards that goal. This prevents becoming overwhelmed, and helps you stay on track.

'Micro-productivity' is the term used to capture the essence of the tried-and-true wisdom of breaking goals down into smaller tasks. It's far easier to focus on taking small steps one at a time rather than looking with dread at the entire marathon distance ahead of you. A large, seemingly overwhelming task can sometimes be transformed into a set of smaller, more manageable micro-tasks that can each be accomplished independently. Breaking tasks into micro-tasks results in longer overall task completion times, but higher quality outcomes and a better experience that may be more resilient to interruptions (Cheng et al., 2015).

So, what exactly makes this small distance vs marathon distance strategy so helpful for all of us? It has to do with working memory, which is used in mental tasks.

Workplace productivity coach, Dr Melissa Gratias, explains that memory limits vary slightly from person to person, but our average working memory capacity is only up to five items. Anything more than that is unlikely to be remembered. If we were to rely on our memory, we would stop at every step of the task to remember what we needed to do next. Each pause is an opportunity to get distracted, or worse, miss a step (Melissa Gratias, 2020).

Breaking a more extensive project down into smaller steps helps us to identify what action to take next. Importantly, this shouldn't happen mentally – we know that memories are not that great! These need to be recorded somewhere to come back to later.

We also work better with specific goals. Let's say you set a goal to write a book (I've been there!). In reality, that's a pretty vague objective. What kind of book? When does it need to be published? How will you make this happen? Specificity is one of the core elements of goal-setting theory, established by psychologist Edwin Locke in the late 1960s.

Gary Latham and Edwin Locke (2015) published a few reasons why specific goals are so powerful:

- *They force us to choose to pursue them and exclude anything irrelevant, increasing our focus and a sense of purpose in pursuing that goal.*

- *They incite effort, which is another cornerstone of motivation.*

- *They also inspire us to be persistent because we have a clear idea of what success looks like.*

Latham cited that those specific goals immediately get us acting on the strategies necessary to attain them.

How does all of this relate to micro-productivity? Breaking a large project down to bite-sized tasks allows you to set far more specific milestones and, as a result, keep you motivated and moving in the right direction.

Big projects can take years. These are the mental marathons I spoke about at the start of this book. There's nothing more frustrating than investing work into a task, only to discover at a much later date that you were not on track. Another reason why micro-productivity is crucial is that you obtain the opportunity to receive feedback and adjust when necessary.

How does this workout improve strength?

Breaking goals down into smaller micro-tasks gives us a sense of purpose and direction, gives us courage because smaller tasks seem manageable and increase confidence! Small steps help you fly through obstacles. Over time, you cultivate an appreciation for improvements as they happen. Your successes become the foundations for more success, and slowly you make a permanent change. Marathons are won one step at a time, not all in one go.

When should you consider doing this workout?

If you're feeling overwhelmed by the size or timeframe of your goal. If you feel demotivated. If you're not making progress. If you feel doubt about your progress.

Instructions

Step 1: Review the deadline

Review the deadline for your main goal. If your deadline is 6 months from now, you have 180 days to complete the objective.

Step 2: Allocate an actionable step

Allocate each day with an actionable step – these are micro-projects! Take out a piece of paper, or open a spreadsheet such as Excel, and create 180 spaces – one for each day of the following 6 months. How? Think of what you'll need, what you'll need to learn, where you will recruit support.

Here's an example of six sub-goals that will allow you to achieve the goal of writing a book:

1. *Choose a book title.*
2. *Decide on theme.*
3. *Create a chapter structure.*
4. *Name each chapter.*
5. *Research Chapter 1.*
6. *Research Chapter 2.*

Step 3: Do one micro-project today!

You now know which step of your micro-project you can take this very day to move you closer to your goal.

Workout 2: Recruit support

What is the workout?

Do you have a hard time asking for help? This is a common problem. People are often resistant to reaching out to others for help, whether it's for help with a project or support with personal stress. My theory for why this happens is that we're afraid that others will think less of us. Or perhaps we're scared of looking imperfect or of being rejected. Other times, we may feel awkward about inconveniencing someone else with our problems. Most people would instead give help than receive it.

The reality is that we all have limitations. No-one can do it all. No-one. We all need someone, sometimes. When we attempt to do everything on our own, we miss out on an opportunity to build a connection with another person. And it can be quite a compliment to ask someone else for their help. Think about when you've given support before, and someone graciously received it.

Often, consulting a trusted friend or advisor can help you gain perspective because that person may not be as emotionally invested as you. They can offer a more objective opinion, giving you more options to consider. Michelle's story shows how she uses the strengths of others to help her make decisions.

How does this workout improve strength?

Having a support network increases your courage. A study published in 2014 showed that when we feel that we have social support, we can cope successfully with life's adversities and actively pursue life opportunities for growth and development (Feeney and Collins, 2014). Even the best heroes have sidekicks. How good does it feel to go into battle with someone you trust by your side?

When should you consider doing this workout?

When you feel stuck or unsure of your choices. If you feel negative or are lacking confidence.

Instructions

Step 1: Determine what help you need

It will be more helpful if you know what you need support for exactly. Spend 5 minutes clarifying which areas you need assistance in. In this way, you can be more specific when recruiting someone's help or advice.

Step 2: Get clear on who could help you

Create a list of names of people who may be able to help you. They could be family members, colleagues, mentors, coaches or friends. Match each person with your specific needs. You must find the right person for their help. Do they have the ability, knowledge or time to help you with your problem?

Step 3: Set the date

Don't delay – set a date to meet your support person. Ask to meet the person you've selected as soon as possible. Don't procrastinate. Act!

Step 4: Pick up the phone and ask

If you can't meet them directly, just call and ask for help. Be direct – don't drop hints, sigh or look sad. Clearly explain what you need help with. Don't waffle or apologise for needing help. Don't say, 'I know you're busy, so only if you have time… only if you want to… sorry, I know this is a lot to ask…' Talking like this infers that you don't consider yourself, your time or the request to be valuable. Instead, say, 'I need help with… would you be able to?' This way, the person is clear about what to help you with and when to help you.

Workout 3: Avoid worry

What is the workout?

Michelle told us how she deals with her constant worry. She permits herself time to worry and thinks her way through it, rather than avoids it. David Carbonell wrote a fantastic book called *The Worry Trick*. In it, he says that anxiety is a powerful force since it makes us question our decisions and ourselves, and causes us to worry about the future. Stress and worry fill our days with dread and emotional turbulence and convinces us there's danger ahead. It then tricks us into getting into fight, flight, or freeze mode – even when there's no danger. Carbonell goes on to discuss how to tackle worry if you're a habitual worrier.

The workout below is a shortened version of one of his techniques. Carbonell explains that worries are not based on what's likely to happen. Worries are based on what would be terrible if it did happen. It's not about probability but actually on fear. Rather than encouraging you to avoid or resist worry, the techniques in Carbonell's book show you how avoidance can make anxiety worse. I would strongly urge you to read this book if you're a chronic worrier. The workout here helps you on the occasions where worry pops up over something happening in your life at a given time.

How does this workout improve strength?

This workout increases your sense of control and courage so that you can find ways to influence the outcome of your goals. A strong mind works through feelings of fear and inadequacy and focuses on reaching the goal. When you can locate the smaller problems within a more significant situation, we're less likely to feel out of control.

When should you consider doing this workout?

When you find yourself ruminating over the worst possible outcomes or failures. When you're experiencing doubt. When you're experiencing fear or worry.

Instructions

Step 1: Select a 'worry time'

Set aside a window of 'worry time' every day. Try a variety of times and stick with one that works best for you.

Step 2: Do nothing but worry for 10 minutes

This may seem counterintuitive, but, give yourself 10 minutes to do nothing but worry. Don't fight the worry. Allow it to flow for a full 10 minutes. You'll be surprised at how difficult this is after 5 minutes. When you resist your worries, you generally worry more. When you give yourself time to do nothing but worry, you find you worry less.

Step 3: Speak your greatest worry out loud

During your worry time, allow your mind to exaggerate the worst possible outcome of your concern. Now speak it out loud to yourself. You'll start to hear how silly your worry is.

Step 4: Get on with your day

Now that you've completed the dedicated time to worry, get on with your day. Your worry may pop up again, but continue without fighting it and it should pass much faster

7

Endurance Training

'He who has a "why" to live for can bear almost any "how".

Friedrich Nietzsche, 1844–1900,
German philosopher

IcanDO Consulting is the brainchild of Tania Plakonouris. It's a reflection of her passion for the development and empowerment of people. IcanDO Consulting mobilises individuals, companies, and institutions to create widespread social change. They focus on leveraging financial and human capital towards a greater good by partnering with the private and corporate sectors to reinvent patterns of patronage to better support local communities.

Tania was born and raised in Johannesburg, South Africa. Her deep appreciation for nature led her to complete a degree in nature conservation through UNISA, which she passed with distinction. She managed a series of children's environmental education programmes for Heritage Hotels in Kenya, and coordinated the opening of three hotels across Kenya and South Africa.

The No 5 Boutique Art Hotel, which Tania managed for 5 years, won numerous awards in South Africa's hospitality sector. Her hospitality experience also includes management of the premier lodge at the prestigious Shamwari Game Reserve. She's since owned and operated two successful businesses in Port Elizabeth.

In 2015, Tania transitioned into the field of NGOs, taking on the position of Programme Manager of the Youth Development Programme for Wilderness Foundation Africa. Her consistent efforts did not go unnoticed, and she was a finalist in the corporate and social category of the Regional Business Achiever Awards in Port Elizabeth, in 2012 and 2018.

Tania has created much success for herself. Yet when I asked Tania to tell me about a single meaningful goal she'd pursued, she responded that her main goal is to find 'the purpose of life' and 'pursue happiness'. She says that through her purpose, her goals are born. And it is clear from her experiences why she has lived true to this goal.

Tania says that her pursuit of happiness and internal peace has only been evident to her in the last 12 years. Before that, she'd gone through life pretty much carefree and oblivious to how precious time is. There was a mindset shift when she became a mother. Her goal of achieving internal peace has never been so important to her as when she realised her daughters watch her every move. So she sets 'daily little adventures' for herself. This includes keeping healthy, staying up-to-date with general knowledge, making sure she does one or two daily random acts of kindness for strangers or friends or family and maintaining her relationship with her husband, Ryan.

As a result, Tania says her 'standout' achievements are that she's climbed Mt Kenya and managed to swim 3 km non-stop. She also reads at least one book a month and one blog of interest per day and has raised funds for under-resourced youths to attend school and hasn't been afraid to ask what Ryan would expect from his partner and delivering it.

What obstacles did Tania encounter? She says there's a persistent voice in her head that wants her to see problems rather than possibilities. She adds that it's effortless to look at the glass half empty rather than the glass half full. But she soon realised that the physical obstacles were not the issue. A lack of money, owning the wrong brand of shoe, having a flabby tummy or working with an annoying colleague are not the problems. The most significant obstacles, she says, are the ones you only feel inside you and that only you can witness and hear.

Tania tries to see the opportunities around her every day. But it all depends if the positive Tania or the negative Tania wants to see the opportunities daily.

Tania says, 'So, what I mean is that the same set of opportunities come your way daily, but it is up to you to keep your arms wide open to accept them. The opportunities are dependent on making themselves visible only if you give them the authority to do so. Opportunities are a series of activities you decide to invite into you. My opportunities are defined as gratitude, giving and willingness. They are sometimes in disguise, but it depends on your internal peace to have the ability to recognise them.' Tania deals with her negative emotions daily and invites her faith to join her. Her deep faith assists her in finding quiet places and have conversations with God.

Tania adds that she's very clear on her values, which she states are kindness, tolerance, patience, and having a helpful and non-judgmental disposition. She says that if she has lived by these values, her goal is achieved daily, but she knows she has to work on it to maintain the status of 'achieved'.

Looking back, Tania says that a big lesson for her has been to learn that everyone is resilient, yet we need to master enabling resilience in our lives. Here are Tania's tips for encouraging resilience in your life:

- *Be optimistic – treat yourself in a loving way, because you can trust yourself more, and your confidence grows. When it becomes easier to trust yourself and others, your trust in the goodness of life grows too.*

- *Learn to forgive – forgiving is an act of kindness to yourself. One of the main obstacles for forgiving someone who's wronged you is the feeling that the other person would get off quickly. It doesn't work that way. To a large extent, we forgive for our benefit instead of for the other person.*

- *Look after yourself – be disciplined enough to exercise and rest.*

- *Learn to problem solve – be focused, assertive, ambitious and future-minded. Do constructive analysis and learn to improvise.*

- *Maintain healthy relationships – we can all learn to grow our social selves by exploring three essential facts: kindness makes you healthy, empathy is something you can learn, and you build relationships by investing in trust.*

The difference between endurance, resilience and enduring

People often confuse endurance with resilience. The difference is that endurance is the measure of a person's stamina or persistence, while according to the American Psychological Association, resilience is the process of adapting well in the face of adversity, trauma, tragedy, threats or even significant sources of risk.

If you've ever run a marathon, you know that you need to train for endurance. To run 42.2 km takes most people an average of 4 hours. Your muscles need to be able to withstand holding you upright and in the same position for that time. That is endurance. It would help if you also had the resilience to run a marathon. How quickly you recover allows you to get back to training afterwards.

In the same way, your endurance and resilience need to be present when undertaking a meaningful long-term goal. It would be best if you had the endurance to go the distance and resilience to help you deal with setbacks.

We breed the misconception of resilience versus endurance from childhood. Parents teach their children resilience by celebrating when their child stays up until 3 am to study for an exam when, in fact, this is endurance rather than resilience.

Then there's the way people think enduring through the pain with a brave face is resilience. If you're resilient, you don't need to 'endure' for the sake of looking strong for others. Instead, resilience can be seen as having good outcomes despite high risk, competence under stress, recovery from stress, and using challenges for growth that makes future hardships more manageable. People will often say they're resilient, when, in fact, they're merely enduring suffering until they break under pressure.

Resilience means 'bouncing back' from difficulty. Research shows that resilience is not an extraordinary phenomenon. In 2012, Steven Southwick and his colleagues studied three highly resilient groups of people: former Vietnam prisoners of war, Special Forces instructors, and men and women who had endured other terrible situations. They analysed these groups on five different levels. Those levels were genetic, psychological, biological, social and spiritual (Southwick, 2012).

Before going forward with the research, Southwick believed resilient people were 'rare and possibly genetically gifted'. They turned out to be wrong (Southwick, 2012). They found out that resilience is common and that anyone can train themselves to be more resilient. Ordinary people commonly demonstrate resilience. It's important to note that levels of resilience change and develop throughout our lives. At times, we may not cope as well as other times. Or we surprise ourselves when we manage a particularly difficult situation. Resilience is just one of many tools we can use to get us back to feeling normal again.

Meaningful goals provide a dynamic tension of just enough stress to challenge and motivate you without overwhelming you. They also offer many opportunities for setback and perceived failure. Being resilient is being able to adapt when something stressful happens. It's the ability to pick ourselves up after a stressful experience.

And endurance is continuing long after you've bounced back.

In this chapter, I've combined workouts that allow you to stay persistent with your goal and help you adapt well to your changing environment in a healthy way. In effect, this chapter is about endurance and resilience combined, like training for and racing in a marathon.

Why are resilience and endurance important in goal-setting?

As we all know, when we feel as if things are about to go from bad to worse, it can be challenging to recover and regain stability.

Resilience in goal-setting has been proven to increase performance. A study on Olympic athletes in 2012 demonstrated the role of resilience in the attainment of optimal performance. The study also discussed how good self-perceptions for peaking under pressure and coping with adversity were factors in performance. In other words, those who perceived they were resilient performed better than others (Fletcher and Sarkar, 2012). Resilience in goal-setting is vital for several reasons. Firstly, it enables us to develop mechanisms to protect us from being overwhelmed. It also helps us to regain balance in our lives during painful periods.

Other benefits of developing resilience are:

- *Improved abilities to learn*
- *Lower rates of absenteeism from work or study due to illness*
- *Fewer risk-taking behaviours like excessive drinking, smoking or drug use*
- *Increased involvement in social activities*
- *A lower mortality rate and increased physical health*

All those benefits will only serve to contribute to you achieving your goals in a healthy way.

Endurance is a more rigid mindset where you continually push yourself to the limit without giving up. It's important to remember the lessons of burnout in previous chapters – endurance is more likely to lead to burnout if not done in a measured and thoughtful way and if you haven't built up your training in this area.

Are there different types of resilience?

You may have heard of 'emotional resilience' before. It refers to how we can manage the emotional impact of stress. However, there are different types of resilience developed and used throughout our lives (Davis-Street et al., 2018).

Inherent resilience

We are all born with this natural resilience. Natural resilience informs how we discover and explore the world and learn to take risks. This occurs significantly within children under the age of about seven (provided their development is not disrupted, and they don't experience any trauma).

Adapted resilience

Adapted resilience occurs at different points in our lives and is brought about through a challenge or crisis. Examples would be going through redundancy at work and then finding the resilience to look for a job the next day. Or experiencing the end of a relationship and finding the confidence to meet someone new. Adaptive resilience needs to be learnt on the spot in a given situation and can give us the ability to manage stress and pain.

Learnt resilience

Learnt resilience is built up over time, and we activate it through painful experiences from our past. We know to draw on it when we experience an unpleasant situation. It's through this resilience that we learn, grow and develop our mechanisms for managing, and find ways to draw on the strength we did not know we had in times when we needed it the most.

There are several ways that we can develop more endurance and resilience. According to psychologist Dr Greg Eells, resilient people have the following traits in common:

- *They have quality social connections and support.*

- *They have the right attitude. They know that bad times don't last, and they don't allow bad experiences to permeate into their whole existence.*

- *They understand their values.*

- *They can label their emotions.*

- *They know how to be silly and have fun, even during tough times (Eells, 2017).*

How many of these could you identify in Tania's story?

Unfortunately, there are many ways you can also undermine your resilience. The following characteristics and habits serve to erode your resilience and endurance over time.

- *Being unable to articulate what your values are and what your vision for the future is*

- *Becoming overwhelmed by emotions*

- *Hiding emotions and pretending that you're fine when you're not*

- *Not seeing opportunities*

- *Thinking that the bad times will never end*

Do you recognise any of these traits in yourself?

There are three workouts for endurance and resilience in this chapter, and they're in linked to the traits, characteristics and habits above. However, any activity that increases the positive traits mentioned will assist you with your resilience and endurance. See if you can create some of your own workouts to develop one of the traits mentioned.

Bibliography

Davis-Street, J., Frangos, S., Walker, B. & Sims, G. (2018). Addressing Adaptive and Inherent Resilience – Lessons Learned from Hurricane Harvey. Society of Petroleum Engineers. Retrieved from https://www.onepetro.org/conference-paper/SPE-190639-MS.

Eells, G.T. (2017). Hyper-Achievement, Perfection, and College Student Resilience, *Journal of College and Character*, 18:2, pp. 77–82. Retrieved from https://www.researchgate.net/publication/316816858_Hyper-Achievement_Perfection_and_College_Student_Resilience

Fletcher, D. & Sarkar, M. (2012). A grounded theory of psychological resilience in Olympic champions. *Psychology of Sport and Exercise*, 13(5), pp. 669–678. Retrieved from https://www.sciencedirect.com/science/article/pii/S1469029212000544.

Frankl, V. (1963). *Man's Search for Meaning*. New York: Pocket Books.

Fredrickson, B. (2001). The role of positive emotions in positive psychology: The broaden-and-build theory of positive emotions. *American Psychologist*, 56(3), pp. 218–226. Retrieved from https://psycnet.apa.org/doiLanding?doi=10.1037%2F0003-066X.56.3.218.

Parrott, W. G. (2002). The functional utility of negative emotions. In L. F. Barrett & P. Salovey (Eds.) The wisdom in feeling: Psychological processes in emotional intelligence (pp. 341–359). New York: The Guilford Press.

Seligman, M. (2011). *Learned Optimism*. North Sydney, NSW: William Heinemann Australia.

Southwick, S. & Charney, D. (2012). The Science of Resilience: Implications for the Prevention and Treatment of Depression. *Science*, 338(6103), pp.79–82. Retrieved from https://www.researchgate.net/publication/232220977_The_Science_of_Resilience_Implications_for_the_Prevention_and_Treatment_of_Depression.

Vine, V. & Aldao, A. (2014). Impaired Emotional Clarity and Psychopathology: A Transdiagnostic Deficit with Symptom-Specific Pathways through Emotion Regulation. *Journal of Social and Clinical Psychology*, 33(4), pp. 319–342. Retrieved from http://d-scholarship.pitt.edu/33229.

Workouts for Endurance and Resilience

Workout 1: Align actions to long-term vision and values

What is the workout?

Psychologist Victor Frankel wrote a compelling book called *Man's Search for Meaning*. In it, he describes his experiences in German concentration camps during World War II. He recounts the story where after choosing not to escape the concentration camp and stay with his patients his 'unhappy feeling' left him, and he 'gained an inward peace' he'd never experienced before. He was able to align his difficult and stressful and traumatic experience to his values, and this made all the difference (Frankl, 1963).

You are guided by what it is you want to achieve. Having clarity in your values and vision allows for decisiveness when facing tough choices, and for you to maintain perspective when you feel overwhelmed. No matter your goal, what's important is being specific and clear.

This workout is about finding out what motivates you. In Tania's story, we see that what motivates her are her values and her drive to find happiness. She's also driven by being an excellent example for her daughters. Take a moment to think about what drives you to persevere in your day-to-day life. Do you share characteristics with Tania? Or do other motivations inspire you? What would you do with your time if you didn't have to worry about primary concerns like money? You may find that your motives are closely linked to your values. For instance, if you value friendship, you might be motivated to spend time with the friends you already have and meet new people. Therefore, aligning actions or goals to your values will burn you out less, and keep you moving forward.

How does this workout improve endurance?

Clarity

The clarity in your vision and values keeps you focused on staying the course for long periods. Tania has been on her quest for 12 years! That's a long time, and she still finds the endurance and resilience to continue each day. For her, it's not about arriving. It's about the quest itself. It's easy to get distracted by unimportant events if you don't have anything specific to aim at. The actor, Bruce Lee, even famously said, 'A goal is not always meant to be reached, it often serves simply as something to aim at.' That's what having a vision does. It gives you something clear to aim for so that when things get tough, you know what's important to keep you focused.

Congruence

Congruence occurs when all your actions are working together through medium- and short-terms goals. When you don't have a clear vision, some of your goals may conflict. It will result in frustration because moving towards one goal moves you further from the other. What happens next? You give up. Your endurance is diminished.

If your actions are aligned through a clear purpose and vision, every effort slowly moves you towards success. Every step helps you achieve feats that others deem impossible. As mentioned in earlier chapters, understanding your values and aligning them to your goals makes the goal far more meaningful. Think about the difference between setting a goal that's arbitrary compared to a meaningful goal. When the going gets tough, will you be able to continue to pursue your goal without being drained or without giving up?

When should you consider doing this workout?

When you're questioning your reasons for trying to achieve your goal. When you feel fatigued, stressed about the goal or have a lack of motivation.

Instructions

Step 1: Determine your core values

From the following list, choose and write down each core value that resonates with you. If you think of a value you possess that's not on the list, write it down. Group all similar values and choose one word with each group that represents the entire group in a way that makes sense to you. Create a maximum of five groupings. If you have more than five clusters, drop the least essential grouping(s). Choose one word within each group that represents the entire group. Again, don't overthink your labels – there are no right or wrong answers.

Step 2: Group values together

Group all similar values and choose one word with each group that represents the entire group in a way that makes sense to you. Create a maximum of five groupings. If you have more than five clusters, drop the least essential grouping(s). Choose one word within each group that represents the entire group. Again, don't overthink your labels – there are no right or wrong answers.

Step 3: Add verbs to labels

Add a verb to each value label and link to your goals/activities. Let's say your goal is to write a book. You will have many activities that link to this goal. Add a verb to each value so you can see what it looks like as an actionable core value and then attribute it to an activity or your goal.

For example:

- *Live in freedom by only writing for 2 hours a day and leaving the rest of the day free to pursue other things.*

- *Seek opportunities for making a difference by writing a book that helps people.*

- *Act with mindfulness when writing each chapter.*
- *Promote wellbeing in the core message of the book.*

This will guide you in the actions you need to take to feel like you're truly living with purpose.

Abundance	Dedication	Kindness	Resourcefulness
Acceptance	Dependability	Knowledge	Responsibility
Accountability	Diversity	Leadership	Responsiveness
Achievement	Empathy	Learning	Risk-taking
Adventure	Encouragement	Love	Safety
Advocacy		Loyalty	Security
Ambition	Enthusiasm	Making a difference	Self-control
Appreciation	Ethics	Mindfulness	Selflessness
Attractiveness	Excellence	Motivation	Service
Autonomy	Expressiveness	Optimism	Simplicity
Balance	Fairness	Open-mindedness	Spirituality
Being the best	Family	Originality	Stability
Benevolence	Flexibility	Passion	Success
Boldness	Friendships	Performance	Teamwork
Brilliance	Freedom		Thankfulness
Calmness	Fun	Personal development	Thoughtfulness
Caring	Generosity	Peace	Traditionalism
Challenge	Grace	Perfection	Trustworthiness
Charity	Growth	Playfulness	Understanding
Cheerfulness	Happiness	Popularity	Uniqueness
Cleverness	Health	Power	Usefulness
Collaboration	Honesty	Preparedness	Versatility
Community	Humility	Proactive	Vision
Commitment	Humour	Professionalism	Warmth
Compassion	Inclusiveness	Punctuality	Wealth
Consistency	Independence	Quality	Wellbeing
Contribution	Individuality	Recognition	Wisdom
Cooperation	Innovation	Relationships	Zeal
Creativity	Inspiration	Reliability	
Credibility	Intelligence	Resilience	
Curiosity	Intuition		
Daring	Joy		
Decisiveness			

Workout 2: Label emotions

What is the workout?

Culture sanctifies language and tells us that the presence of unpleasant feelings, thoughts, memories, bodily sensations are signals that something is wrong and must change. We believe that healthy living cannot occur until negative experiences are eliminated. This means that we continually fight negative emotions. We try to push them down, avoid them, or hide them.

As an alternative to avoidance, we can actively be aware of and embrace our emotions without trying to change things, especially if attempting to change causes psychological harm. This is the science of positive and negative emotions. Psychology has long understood the value of negative emotions and how anger helps us, how anxiety helps us, and how sadness even can help us (Parrott, 2002). What's important is how those negative emotions affect us.

Martic Seligman describes the 3 Ps as important for resilience. *Personalisation* is thinking that the problem is yourself, instead of considering other outside things that have caused it. Realising outside factors have caused a bad situation allows us to reduce the blame and criticism we put on ourselves. *Permanence* is thinking a bad situation will last forever. Those who think setbacks are temporary have improved ability to accept and adapt for the future. *Pervasiveness* is thinking a bad situation applies across all areas of your life, instead of only happening in one area. People who think bad situations are pervasive feel that all areas of their life are impacted. This can make it hard to carry on (Seligman, 2011). Negative emotions are only bad if you personalise them, if you allow them to be pervasive, and if you think they are permanent.

So what about positive emotions? The leader in the field of positive emotions is a psychologist named Dr Barbara Fredrickson. She's at the University of North Carolina, and she's led our understanding of the benefits of positive emotion. Her theory is called the broaden-and-build theory of positive emotion (Fredrickson, 2001).

Take a minute to generate as many different positive emotion words as you can come up with.

I assume that you chose words such as love, joy, glee, happy, exhilarated, gratitude, contentment, and tranquillity. These are universal positive emotions.

Fredrickson helps us to understand that positive emotions, just like the ones I mentioned – joy, contentment, gratitude and so forth – broaden our attention. They expand our awareness, and they help us to be more creative and more cognitively flexible. Negative emotions narrow your thinking (Fredrickson, 2001). Think about the last time you were angry. Probably, you remember that your attention 'closed'. You may have found yourself ruminating about the transgression, thinking about the person that transgressed you. Your energy and your thoughts probably centred on defending yourself and fighting back. The negative emotions narrowed your attention. Positive emotions do the opposite. Positive emotions broaden our awareness and help us to be more creative.

This workout is about regulating and labelling emotions. When faced with conflict or change, the fight-or-flight response of the brain loves to flare up. When you overcome that instinctive emotional response and maintain your composure, you have the space to see opportunities and solve problems in novel ways. Tania mentioned this when I spoke to her. She identifies and regulates her mindset so that she's more open to seeing opportunities rather than threats. She also uses her faith to deal with her negative emotions. Allowing your emotions to take over prevents you from thinking critically.

Interestingly, some people find it more difficult to label their emotions than others. No matter how complex their emotions are, they're still only able to list a small number of labels to describe them. Research by Vine & Aldao in 2014 showed that this impoverished emotional labelling is associated with deficits in regulating those emotions.

Simply put, the less aware we are of our emotions, the less likely we are to regulate them (Vine & Aldao, 2014).

How does this workout improve endurance?

This workout helps you get in touch with your emotions so that you can appropriately label them during future events and, in turn, regulate them. The workout allows you to focus on the 3 Ps. This allows you to maintain composure in the future, rather than be carried away by negative feelings.

The workout will enable you to know when an emotion arises or threatens to sweep away your attention. You'll be able to label it and then return to your work or activity. Composure is not only crucial for dealing with a crisis. It also helps us tackle the little things so that we can be resilient and bounce back. Remember, composure does not equate to 'putting on a brave face'. It's not about enduring through suffering. An example of composure would be not allowing yourself to get angry in a traffic jam because you understand it is not useful. Maintaining composure means staying calm so that you can save your energy for what's important. I mean genuinely feeling peaceful rather than pretending to be.

Furthermore, composure is not only about being able to return to a state of poise. It's also about understanding the beliefs and expectations you had that produced the emotions. For example, if you expected that nothing would ever go wrong with your project, then it's likely you received a big shock. When something did go wrong, you were upset, angry, sad – emotional! Compare that with a more realistic belief that, most likely, something was going to go wrong, and when it did, you managed it.

When should you consider doing this workout?

When you find yourself experiencing negative emotions or when you find yourself hiding your emotions.

Instructions

There are many different meditations that can be found online. The following meditation is a short and simple exercise that requires no special equipment or venue and can be done in short bursts at any time of day.

Step 1: Find a place to sit

Start by finding a comfortable, quiet place to sit in an upright and relaxed posture. You may want to close your eyes or focus on a point just in front of you on the ground. Take three deep and slow breaths.

Step 2: Scan your body

Bring your awareness to different sensations in your body. Notice how your body feels on the chair. Think of the sensations on your finger tips and notice the sensations of your breathing. Don't worry if you become distracted. Acknowledge that your mind has wandered and bring your attention back to your breathing. You may want to count your breaths as a way to focus again.

Step 3: Notice your emotions

As you continue breathing, note the emotions and thoughts you have. Ask yourself what you are feeling in that moment.

Step 4: Label the most prominent emotion or emotions

Try to identify the strongest feeling that you're having and give it a name. It could be longing, joy, relief, or anything else. Repeat that name a few times as you continue to breathe through the exercise. Now return your focus to your breathing and repeat the exercise. You should begin to notice changes in your emotions and labels as you move through the exercise.

Step 5: Open your eyes

Slowly open your eyes if they've been closed during the exercise. Or return your gaze to items around the room.

Workout 3: See new opportunities

What is the workout?

It's a fact that people with low resilience experience permanence. This is where their negative evaluations of an event are seen as ongoing and as though they will never end. They see permanent barriers in their way. A resilient mindset knows that both negative and positive experiences come to an end, and what's more important is the way we see opportunities around us. Tania mentioned this over and over to me when she told me her story.

Creativity and innovative problem-solving are incredibly useful when facing challenges. It's not only about applying critical thinking during a crisis, but also about being proactive and preventing things from going wrong. This is like going to the dentist for a regular clean so that you won't need to go back for a tooth filling later. Opportunities are about taking advantage of things as they come your way, *and* about proactively understanding how things may go wrong and acting ahead of time. High resilience means you welcome a changing environment since it always brings with it hidden opportunities. You don't think of change as a permanent threat and you can look for things that others might have missed, helping you to succeed.

How does this workout improve endurance?

This workout helps you shift your thinking from focusing on barriers to focusing on what can be done instead. It helps you use obstacles as a means to think of creative ways to overcome them so that you can stay the course for longer. When you hit a big bump in the road, you'll find a way to climb over it. Or perhaps you'll find a way around it. You won't just stand there and wonder why you hit the bump or wonder why the bump won't go away, and you'll eventually give up.

When should you consider doing this workout?

When you're faced with barriers or experiencing stress.

Instructions

Step 1: How to move forward

When you find yourself thinking that you're stuck or like you can't do something, reframe the phrase and ask yourself how you can move forward.

Step 2: How to improve the situation

Once you've worked out how you might move forward, a follow-up question is to ask yourself what you can do to improve the situation.

Step 3: Brainstorm your ideas

Mind map or brainstorm your thoughts on paper and choose your best options.

8

Composition Training

'Successful people maintain a positive focus in life no matter what is going on around them. They stay focused on their past successes rather than their past failures, and on the next action steps they need to take to get them closer to the fulfilment of their goals rather than all the other distractions that life presents to them.'

Jack Canfield

On your journey to achieving your goals, the composition of your thoughts is going to take you to the next level. Composition is about what's present in your mindset that stops you from achieving your goals. This could be a lack of confidence. It could be pessimism. It could be negative people in your life telling you that you can't succeed. It could be distractions.

When I asked Johnsen Lim for his official title, he said that he's an architect and also a 'professional dreamer'. Johnsen says he dreams a lot because as long as they're positive and reasonable dreams, they keep him motivated. He dreams of living in an architecturally designed house, having a healthy-looking body, and having the financial freedom. In simple terms, Johnsen says his main goals are the usual trifecta of 'to live healthily, mortgage-free and enjoy my job'.

Two years ago, Johnsen made a significant change to try to make some of his dreams come true. He and his partner moved interstate from Western Australia to a quiet little town in Tasmania. He found a new job, and they moved into a beautiful house overlooking a river. It wasn't long before Johnsen's new employer unfairly changed the conditions of his contract, and he found himself looking for new work. This shattered his plans (and dreams), and he calls it the scariest moment in his life. There's no doubt that when you uproot your life, and it doesn't work out as you had imagined, it can be devastating.

Johnsen says he is lucky to have a very supportive partner. They packed up their home for the second time in a brief period and moved to Sydney. They downsized their home to suit a big city lifestyle and found a compact rental to live in. While this seemed far off from his original dream, Johnsen says that it turned out to be the best decision they made.

Johnsen's reflection on this event is as follows:

'Rejection is not a nice feeling, but everyone experiences rejection and deals with it in different ways. I believe the best way to overcome those challenges is to keep the right people who radiate positivity around you. When times are rough, I find people who cheer me up. I stay away from people who rub salt in the wounds because subconsciously I have the drive to get better. At the time, I didn't know how or what or when I would reach my goal, but I sure made the right choice in listening to people who could help me. It took bravery. I'm proud of our willingness to follow our instincts and try new things.'

After moving to Sydney, Johnsen experienced some new challenges. With diligence, he'd previously managed to lose 8 kg and felt good about his healthy lifestyle. But when he started his new job, the role was very challenging, and he began to doubt himself. He wondered if he'd made the right career move and whether he could keep his cool during tough challenges. His diet changed, and he fell back to old habits. His body reacted poorly, and on top of working long hours, his poor diet caused him to develop fatigue-related symptoms like ulcers, cold sores and other infections. Johnsen said, 'I looked like the walking dead. I knew I needed a break. I needed to get out of the country and break my routine.'

So he took some time off overseas, and on his return, colleagues were genuinely happy to have him back at work. Johnsen started to regain his self-confidence. He used positive affirmations like 'I can do this' and 'this is my domain', and soon realised how people appreciated his role. Today, Johnsen is back on track with his trifecta goals. He's at the gym and feeling healthy, and things have come full circle for him.

I asked Johnsen to share his most important lesson from his experiences. He says, 'Time has a way of fixing things. Time gives you clarity and a chance to think through all your options. Time certainly helped me reorder my priorities.'

Focus from distractions

Johnsen's story reminds us that we are vulnerable to our negative thoughts, through being overwhelmed, or through the opinions of others. He also shows us that we have the power and control to turn that around and to choose who we have in our lives and choose how we view our situations. For me, the composition of a great mindset is a focus from distractions, realistic optimism, and confidence.

Focus is the ability to say *I'm doing this right now and nothing else, and nobody's going to stop me*. A focused mind will do what it plans no matter what anyone says and no matter what happens. Sadly, focus is a casualty of the 21st century. People are consumed with social media and devices. Notifications pop up everywhere – on desktops, phones, watches, and tablets. Those notifications carry with them opinions, constant 'likes', information, and comments. And they all litter minds with doubts and approvals. Instead of commanding their day, people are controlled by distraction.

Distraction is the drug of choice today and supply is endless. It numbs us to the difficulties of facing a challenge. Distractions are easy! Far easier than working through something that's proving to be complicated. How many times do you pick your phone up during the day? Minds wander, become pessimistic, and become disheartened.

In his book *Indistractable*, Nir Eyal describes why solving the problem is not as simple as swearing off our devices. Abstinence is impractical and often makes us want more. He goes on to provide simple strategies for beating distractions, which includes making time for traction and understanding your triggers (Eyal, 2019). If you're working on a goal and have tasks laid out in front of you, it's time to get strategic with how you will prevent distractions. This is where you use the weapons of time, location and mindset. Ask yourself:

- *What time is best to focus on this activity?*
- *Where is the best place for me to focus?*
- *How will you respond to distractions? How will you prevent them?*

Focus is simple, but not easy. It takes a strategy. And it takes commitment to see one thing through to the end at the cost of all other possibilities. Distractions are not your boss. You control them, not the other way around. The more you practise composition and staying focused, the easier it will become.

Realistic optimism

There's a spectrum of ways to think about the future. There are realistic thoughts and unrealistic thoughts, and these are divided into optimism and pessimism (Schneider, 2001). Take a look at the diagram below.

Unrealistic Pessimism	Realistic Pessimism	Realistic Optimism	Unrealistic Optimism

On the extreme left, we have unrealistic pessimism. This is exaggerated negative thinking. People who are unrealistic pessimists imagine that all sorts of irrational catastrophes will ensue from a minor setback. They make mountains from molehills, and their thoughts are generally unhelpful since they are unable to see opportunities.

On the extreme right, we have unrealistic optimism. This is unbridled positive thinking. People who are unrealistic optimists believe that only good things will happen to them. Irrationally, they think that they will be wildly successful in every endeavour. This is also unhelpful because they're unable to foresee risk.

In the middle of the spectrum, there are healthier approaches. These are far more grounded in reality and these are two sides to the same coin.

Realistic pessimism is an accurate assessment of reality and imagines probable outcomes. Pessimism means someone will pay special attention to the bad things that may happen. They give extra weight to the consideration of risks. This can be helpful in situations where risk-assessment is critical, but not in cases where reaching personal goals and growing as a person is required.

This is because a realistic pessimist is afraid of trying something new and leaving their comfort zone. They're good at seeing the obstacles but struggle to see a way around them. Their views discourage hard work because thinking that they will probably fail, this makes them wonder why they should bother. They have a great fear of losing and would instead not try than fail. They tend to believe the excuses their mind generates, and it encourages them to be rather lazy at times. They are more likely to have a fixed mindset and see their abilities and skills as fixed. Realistic pessimists don't recognise that by working through an obstacle, one can improve their skills and expand their options. Their view is limited to what is possible right now, and they fail to imagine later possibilities. As a result, they remain stuck.

On the flip side of the coin, realistic optimists take an accurate assessment of reality and imagine probable outcomes. Their views do not give risk any particular weight, and they are therefore less afraid of losing and less risk-averse. They foresee obstacles, and they also imagine ways to overcome them. Realistic optimists have a growth mindset. They believe in their own ability to learn and grow. They guess what can happen and work hard to make it happen (Schneider, 2001).

Both of these realistic views are self-fulfilling prophecies. They both prove themselves right because both their options are realistic. But one view of the world can hold you back. What sets realistic optimism apart is that it both inspires and depends upon hard work. There's an inherent belief in realistic optimists that they'll succeed if they work hard. This encourages them to put in the persistent effort and to stay focused on the task at hand. They sometimes fail or experience setbacks, but they get back up. As they search for better ways of doing and being, they improve, and goals that seemed out of reach before suddenly become attainable.

This is where someone may ask why being a super-duper optimist doesn't work. Unrealistic optimists are characterised by loving vision boards and act that if they think positively, they will attract good results. Ultimately, it discourages hard work. If all you have to do is visualise the future, why would you put in any effort? Why try if all you have to do is believe that you can succeed. Unfortunately, there's no easy road to success.

Where do you think Johnsen sits on the pessimism/optimism spectrum? I see many traits of realistic optimism. He understood the risks in his choices and took the plunge regardless. He experienced setbacks with some of his goals, yet persisted and improved. He saw opportunities, rather than obstacles. And he's persisting with his dreams.

Maintaining realistic optimism means avoiding feeling sorry for yourself or telling yourself a situation is hopeless. It means looking for ways to take control and dismissing the negative thoughts that stop you from taking action. Realistic optimists ask 'What can I do about this?' Johnsen's story perfectly illustrated this for us. When his situation in Tasmania took a turn for the worst, he stepped back and found solutions. Sure, they weren't what he'd imagined, but they did give him options. And the result was that he ended up in an even better situation. His story also shows that self-talk can be a mischievous source of negativity, so keep an eye on it. If you see that you're giving yourself unhelpful feedback, change it to something positive instead. Johnsen's positive affirmations began to move him forward through his doubts.

There's no doubt that it's challenging to choose to put in hard work without any guarantee of success. It's easier to not go to the gym. It's easier to turn on the TV or surf Facebook than to focus on improving. Is that satisfying, though? You decide!

Confidence

Confidence takes many forms. If I asked you to name someone confident, you might think of someone who's arrogant than someone who has quiet self-assurance. And you may think of people who are like ducks on a pond. Calm on the outside, but underwater, their legs are paddling furiously. The 'fake it till you make it' notion of confidence is different to real confidence. That type of false confidence is projected to mask insecurities. Those people often allow their faith to be shattered by the thoughts and opinions of others. Genuinely confident people stay ahead because they make things happen without worrying about what other people think or say. Other's opinions are not distractions.

I think Henry Ford said it best: 'Whether you think you can, or you think you can't – you're right.'

Learning to be truly confident, and not faking it, is essential.

Thankfully, with a few subtle changes in the way you think (and a little help from neuroscience), you can get your wandering and pessimistic mind to stay in 'the zone' and focus better. Composition training is about having the right mental muscles to stay focused on the tasks at hand and to maintain confidence and realistic optimism as you go.

What undermines composition?

The following habits and characteristics undermine focus, optimism and confidence:

- *Seeing only the barriers and risks in a situation*

- *Not letting go of failure and negative experiences*

- *Being overly concerned with the thoughts and opinions of others*

Do you recognise any of these traits in yourself? If yes, consider one or more of the workouts on the following pages

Bibliography

Eyal, N. (2019). *Indistractable: How to Control Your Attention and Choose Your Life.* London: Bloomsbury Publishing.

Gu, J., Strauss, C., Bond, R. & Cavanagh, K. (2015). How do mindfulness-based cognitive therapy and mindfulness-based stress reduction improve mental health and wellbeing? A systematic review and meta-analysis of mediation studies. *Clinical Psychology Review*, 37(37), pp. 1–12. Retrieved from https://sciencedirect.com/science/article/pii/s0272735815000197.

Seligman, M. (2011). *Learned Optimism.* North Sydney, NSW: William Heinemann Australia.

Schneider, S. (2001). In search of realistic optimism: Meaning, knowledge, and warm fuzziness. *American Psychologist*, 56(3), pp. 250–263. Retrieved from https://www.ncbi.nlm.nih.gov/pubmed/11315251.

Workouts for Composition

Workout 1: Realistic optimism

What is the workout?

Realistic optimism means not allowing yourself to get too attached to unpleasant events. In his book *Learned Optimism*, Dr Martin Seligman (2011) suggests taking your mind off the situation by doing something enjoyable. This can get you into a better state of mind for looking for solutions. When you're more collected, revisit the unresolved situation. Doing this helps you think of better and more creative solutions.

How does the workout improve composition?

Negative thoughts rob our time and attention. Essentially, extra space in your mind helps you focus on solutions. We've all tried at some point to block pessimistic thoughts. But sadly, the more you try to prevent them, the more they come back. Neuroscience tells us to stop and change up the scenery around you. This will help reframe your thinking and get you focused on something new. Realistic optimism is the ongoing process of exploring the opportunities and challenges, planning to minimise risk and making it work. More importantly, the pursuit of cultivating realistic optimism lies in the journey, not the destination. It allows us to focus our energy into activities that are more likely to bring us success, rather than on trying to stop events that probably won't happen.

When should you consider doing this workout?

Try this workout if you find yourself continually ruminating on negative thoughts and pessimistic or cynical distractions.

Instructions

Step 1: Stop what you are doing

Take a few deep breaths and change rooms, or go outside.

Step 2: Go for a mini-walk

Find a short span of time to go for a short walk. Some of the greatest philosophers and thinkers were avid walkers. Philosopher Friedrich Nietzsche was a mountain climber! By using walks to clear their minds and create space for their thoughts, those thinkers came up with some beautiful ideas.

Step 3: Return and refocus

Get back to work, having cleared your mind – refocus on your tasks for the day.

Workout 2: Declutter and let go

What is the workout?

A strong mind is an uncluttered mind, and so we must stop allowing ourselves to get carried away by unnecessary worries and distractions. It means staying present and focused. Mindful meditation is an excellent way to learn to control your mind.

For many, meditation seems a daunting task and people often turn away from this as a solution. My workout is simple, and with time, it may make it easier for you to practise a full mindfulness session. It takes 5 or 10 minutes a day to start achieving results. If this gets you on track, I recommend one of the many apps to help you get started into a full mindfulness practise.

How does the workout improve composition?

A study published in *Clinical Psychology Review* in 2015 showed that there was consistent evidence that mindfulness improves cognitive and emotional reactivity, and decreases rumination and worry (Gu et al., 2015). Practising mindfulness allows you to stay focused on one activity at a time. Removing distractions, worries, and unhelpful thoughts enables your mind to focus attention on meaningful goals and pursuits when you need to.

When should you consider doing this workout?

If you often do several things at a time, it becomes your default habit. Your lack of productivity will also become a default pattern for you. Try this workout if you'd like to improve your focus. It will train your brain to focus on one thing at a time. Practice this every day and then test yourself. Can you eat an entire meal without checking your social media pages or email? Can you be fully present when someone is talking to you? While working on something, can you spot the distractions as they come?

Instructions

Step 1: Select a new piece of music

Choose some music that's entirely new for you. You may have something in your collection that you've never heard, or you might choose to turn the radio on.

Try not to judge the music by its genre, title or artist name before it's begun. Ignore any labels and neutrally allow yourself to get lost in the sound journey for the duration of the song.

Step 2: Immerse yourself in the music

Close your eyes and put on your headphones Allow yourself to explore every aspect of the music track. Let go of any dislike or like for the piece and exist inside the track.

Step 3: Listen to the dynamics of each instrument

Explore the song by listening to the dynamics of each instrument. Separate each sound in your mind and analyse each one by one.

Step 4: Hone in on the vocals

Hone in on any vocals in the music. Pay attention to the sound of the voice. If there's more than one voice, separate them as you did in Step 3. The idea is to listen intently. Don't think, hear.

Workout 3: Protect against naysayers

What is the workout?

Naysayers are people who discourage you from pursuing your goals and dreams. They could be someone who thinks what you're doing is silly, or even impossible. They could be someone who sabotages you while you're trying to cultivate a new habit – like offering you a cigarette when you're trying to quit smoking. They may even mean well, trying to protect you from setbacks. They may be realistic pessimists! Naysayers, in whatever form, keep you from achieving your highest potential.

You will also need to develop your confidence so that you don't doubt yourself every time someone tells you something you disagree with.

To be more confident in your opinions, you'll need to work on developing a clear perception of others. This workout helps you consider the ideas of trustworthy and admirable people. It lets you discard the thoughts of potentially selfish people with sinister motives that can make you feel confused.

If you notice the person continues to try to persuade you and you have a bad feeling about them, you have the choice to not associate with them anymore. They most likely don't have your best interest at heart.

How does the workout improve composition?

The people you spend time with can profoundly impact your thoughts. Johnsen recognises this in his story and says that he only keeps people in his life who have similar values and thinking. If you notice pessimistic or negative people in your life, you may want to spend less time with them. This is for the sake of your personal growth. Usually though, once you identify some of the 'useless' thoughts they're giving you, you can stop them. By not getting caught up in what others think, you allow yourself not to be distracted by negative thoughts or pessimism.

When should you consider doing this workout?

Consider this workout if you find yourself worrying about someone else's opinion about your goal or ideas.

Instructions

Step 1: Find a quiet place

Find a quiet place to reflect briefly. Make sure it's an area where you will not be interrupted and where you can relax.

Step 2: Evaluate the person

To evaluate the person whose opinion or ideas are worrying you, ask yourself the following questions:

- *Is this person living a life that matches my values?*
- *Has this person achieved success on the subject they're commenting on?*
- *Does this person have knowledge and expertise in the subject they're commenting on?*

Step 3: Evaluate the words they are using

To evaluate their words, ask yourself the following questions:

- *Does this resonate with me and my thoughts?*
- *Are the comments valid?*

- - *Will applying this advice make me better off?*

- - *Are they coming from a place of fear or love?*

Step 4: Decide on the worthiness of the ideas

Decide whether the ideas from this person are worth or not. If the person does indeed have something important to say and adds value through their skills, knowledge and previous accomplishments, perhaps it's is time to look at your perspective. If not, discard their opinions and move on.

Part 3
Mindset Fitness Benefits

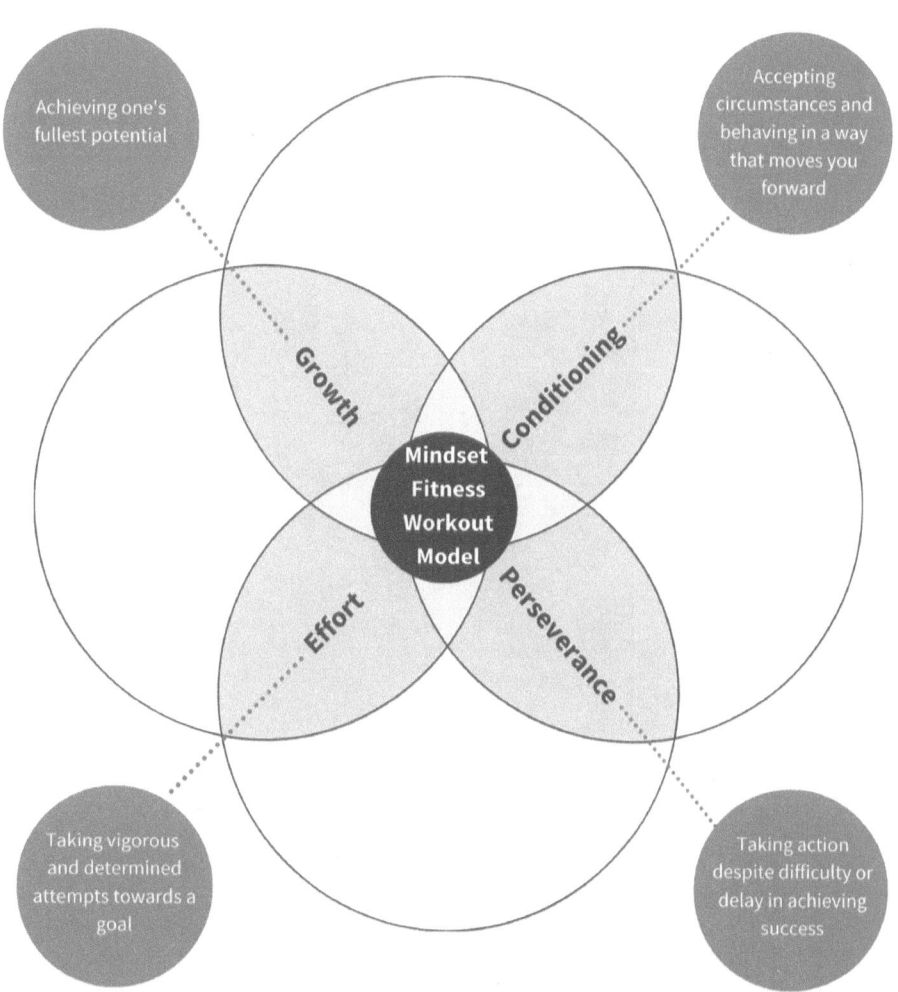

9

The Benefits of the Mindset Fitness Workouts

As with any exercise regiment, you are bound to notice results when you stick to the program and maintain discipline. Little and often is better than occasionally doing a significant amount. Comparable to fitness in the body, the Mindset Fitness Workout is designed to make your mind fit for change and the mental marathons of today. Firstly, the composition of your thoughts will change. Then your perseverance and willpower will improve. The workouts will also help you put in maximum effort without burning out. They're designed to keep you pursuing your goals and moving forward with purpose.

Finally, you're bound to experience an immense amount of personal growth. This comes from achieving personal goals and learning from your experiences as you continue to set new goals and see success.

Conditioning

When we talk about conditioning the body, it's the process of training to become physically fit through a regimen of exercise. Mental conditioning is training your mind to become fit enough to accept the circumstances you find yourself in and behave in a way that moves you forward.

We've been conditioning our minds from when we were children. Society and culture programs fixed patterns of thinking into you. This shapes your identity, who you are, and how you see where you fit in the world. These patterns of thought are also programmed into you by your parents, teachers and peers, and they become deeply embedded into your mind and subconscious. As you move through life, they automatically surface.

Whether you like it or not, your conditioning strives to be self-sustaining. Your mind is in constant motion, and the result is the complex pool of thoughts that serve to identify you and help you decide how to live your life.

Conditioning is activated by people, situations, activities and stress. It's the automatic response you have to those events. As a result, you instantly put on the mask required for the situation. Unfortunately, not all our conditioning helps us perform at our best.

To make lasting change and condition your mind to new patterns of thinking, you first need to recognise your fixed mental pattern! Once you've seen and recognised the patterns, you can recondition them and leave the old ways of thinking behind. If you can identify your fixed mental models that are holding you back from achieving your goals, the workouts in this book will help you create new thought patterns. This will dry up the energy you supply to old habits and condition your mindset with new ways of thinking. In this way, your past mental conditioning will gradually lose its power over you and eventually vanish.

We all know that life is unpredictable and that change happens every day. Many of those changes can transform your life. We can't fight the changes that occur around us. We need to cultivate the ability to accept change and build a habit of looking at life through a positive mindset instead of a fixed defeatist one. The Mindset Fitness Workouts will start to shape and condition you to begin embracing obstacles as part of the course and keep you moving forward without unnecessary worry.

Practising flexibility, acceptance, and resilience prepares you to live in this changing world, where you never know what's going to happen next. It's like protecting yourself with a powerful shield. Over the last few years of building my practice and working with clients in many different settings, I've learnt the real power of accepting change and embracing lessons from failures. I witnessed how people and teams were happier when they understood the changes around them and welcomed them instead of continually resisting and trying to keep things the same.

The workouts in this book are designed to condition your mind to accept things that are out of your control, put measures in place for something you can control and that will help you maintain inner peace and happiness. Your responses will no longer be fixed, and you'll be able to embrace your goals and situation wholeheartedly.

Perseverance

I know all too well that training for and racing in a marathon takes perseverance. Any physical activity where your skills and abilities are challenged takes perseverance.

At the time I started writing this chapter, I'd been training to participate in my first ultra-marathon, a distance of 80 km on sandy trails in the Margaret River region of Western Australia. I had, more than once, used the workouts in this book to help me persevere with the training on the sand.

Unfortunately, at the time I sent this book to my publisher, I was told by my doctor to postpone my ultra-training so that I could get some specialist medical treatment for a long-time problem. This was gut wrenching, especially after I'd put in all the work. But my mindset allows me to see that the goal is not out of reach and that I must take a longer and different road to get there. A different mindset would see me giving up on that goal. Perseverance means acting despite difficulty or delay in achieving success. Persistence is your ability to stick with things. It means finishing what you started and working hard despite the obstacles that may arise. Sometimes you need to dig deep to overcome thoughts of giving up. Even when you can put plans and support in place, perseverance is what you need to keep going until the work is done. The pleasure you receive from completing tasks and projects is vital because it helps build your confidence for future success.

The workouts in this book help you recognise when a goal is essential to you and ensures that you don't give up on it accomplishing it, no matter how hard it is or how many times you've failed. You'll stay determined, even if you don't see how things will work out right now. You will look for a way to take one small step forward every day.

Maximum effort

If I asked you to rate on a scale from 1 to 10 the effort you put into achieving a recent goal, what would your score be? Did you achieve the goal? Or did you fall short? If you scored low on that scale, or if you didn't see the results that you wanted to see, it may be because of a lack of maximum effort. The effort you put in towards achieving a goal is a significant key to success. Putting in maximum effort means taking vigorous and determined attempts towards a goal. Sure, it isn't the only thing needed for you to succeed in achieving your goals, but it is required.

Look around you and think of people who complain about their situations or who are always dissatisfied. I would be willing to bet that (all things being equal) a portion of them wouldn't even come close to putting in the same amount of effort to changing their situation as someone else who may have achieved more success.

The fact of the matter is this: everything that you want to achieve or want to change has a price tag on it. You must be willing to give something up to get something else. The price tag may be time, sore muscles, comfort, or sleeping in. As each day passes, we pay for every success, and success comes down to what kind of effort we gave that day. It reminds me of a quote by bestselling author Rory Vaden. He said, 'Success is never owned; it is only rented – and the rent is due every day.'

That's one of my favourite quotes, and it speaks volumes about the amount of effort it takes to separate yourself from those who achieve mediocrity. A couple of years ago, a friend told me that she admired my successes, but it must have come easy to me because clearly, I'm just a motivated person. She went on to say that not everyone (including her) is as motivated as me and it's harder for them. That couldn't have been further from the truth. When I put my mind to a goal, I put in maximum effort. And that effort doesn't only happen when I feel good or when the timing is right. I don't wait for the sun to shine before I go for a run. I get out in the rain, cold, wind, and heat. I put in effort even when I don't feel like it.

I put in the effort when the conditions aren't perfect. This must seem to an outsider that I'm just more motivated and feeling good every day. But successful people pay their rent over and over again. There will be times when things are perfect, and there will be bad times too. The one thing you can control is the effort you put in.

The workouts in this book are designed to keep you focused, flexible, and mentally strong. That will give you the best opportunity to keep putting in the maximum effort every day without burning yourself out.

Personal growth

To me, personal growth always sounds like a simple thing to do, but in my experience, it always happens during the toughest times. It's comfortable to stay the same though it seldom leads to you achieving new things. Everyone has room for growth and going through it helps you uncover a better version of yourself.

Making improvements throughout your life is not about completely reinventing yourself. Instead, it's about achieving just a little more. It could mean excelling at your job or being kind or having a positive impact on someone's day.

Personal growth helps you get excited about life and about how far you've come. I love looking back and comparing who I am today to who I was yesterday. It challenges me to see just how far I can go. Every little success makes you more excited about life. It's exciting to uncover talents you never knew you had, and it's rewarding to learn new things. It helps you be more aware of the sheer amount of opportunities there are in life. It enables you to improve your interactions with others by making you less self-centred and more focused on meaningful relationships.

The Mindset Fitness Workouts that I cover in this book help you to see opportunities and maintain relationships with people who add value to your life.

They help you see new perspectives and challenge the way you think of problems. They help you be grateful for what's around you. All of that will only serve to help you grow as a person.

Conclusion

I want to conclude this book by telling you Adam Kinnest's story. Adam is an experienced group commercial manager and was the founder of Kiwa Techwear, a start-up in the health tech space.

A few years back, Adam went through two profound experiences and lost two important people in his life. The first was his friend Kerry, lost to a 9-year battle with cancer. Kerry was like a brother to Adam, and it was difficult for him to watch Kerry suffer through his illness.

The second person was a young girl who Adam had gotten to know through an annual trip to Cambodia. Adam supports an organisation there that cares for children living with HIV. On the third day of his 2017 visit, a young Grade 5 girl presented in pain at the clinic. She had a significant tooth infection and needed immediate medical attention. Adam was the only person available to get medical care for her, so he took her to the local hospital. Unfortunately, he was turned away, with the doctor saying that he was finished for the day and to bring the girl back in the morning. Adam proceeded to take her to several local dentists to see if they could help. This too didn't work, and they had to return to the village without medical attention being received.

Since Adam was not medically trained, he called on an aunt who is also a nurse, so that she could talk him through how to administer an IV to try to get things under control. Adam spent the next 12 hours by the girl's bedside. The following day, he tried again to get her medical attention. On the way to the hospital, the young girl lost her life while in Adam's arms.

Those experiences left Adam with a need to contribute to the world in a more meaningful way. He set a goal to improve himself to help people. And so Adam decided to take a personal leap and pursue a nursing degree. He wanted to make a difference in people's lives and to be there for them when it mattered the most to them.

This was a difficult decision for Adam because he had a prior lack of education and still needed to maintain full-time employment while undertaking the degree. His first step was to have the confidence to turn up and make it work.

Those weren't his only obstacles. Since he was in a female-dominated field, he faced ongoing discrimination from fellow students, staff and others who struggled to see Adam as an equal or take him seriously. He was asked on more than one occasion if he was lost on the nursing campus, and was always the lone male voice, and was often neglected.

However, Adam says that experiences from his youth taught him valuable lessons. Having grown up in foster care and feeling discarded and abandoned for most of his young life, he says:

'Only I am in control of the outcomes of my life. Every person struggles, every person has a story or has had something bad happen to them, but I made a choice not to be a victim. I chose to stand up and be me, to stop making excuses and own my life and everything that comes with it, including the bad stuff. My whole life I've had people tell me that I'm worthless, that I won't amount to anything. I wanted to prove the naysayers wrong.'

His experiences on campus only served to motivate Adam further and inspired him to change his path. He's still pursuing the same goal of helping others but wants to do so in a different way. He's now the commercial manager for Gemstar, as well as for Manning & Co, and he's started units on an MBA.

Gemstar is an international education and training company focused on unearthing and helping fast-growth start-ups, scale-ups and SMEs to expand into ASEAN or Australia. Adam's role involves him developing and managing a cross-functional team to support the operations of this international business. As part of the growth of Gemstar, he also took on a role as a program facilitator for an entrepreneurial skills program for the deaf and hard of hearing community.

When I asked Adam about this change, he said, 'At first I struggled when I chose to refocus my goal, thinking I was failing and that I was letting myself down. But I had people around me that gave me good feedback and supported me through the thought process. This gave me the confidence to refocus my goal onto a new path but still see the outcome as achieving my goal of helping people who need it the most. The goals I set myself are directly linked to who I am and my values. This is something that's taken me time to understand, but I value transparency, honesty, hard work, passion and purpose.' So, while Adam didn't achieve becoming a nurse, he is undoubtedly achieving his goal of helping people.

Adam goes on to say that he loves to set big goals, and while he doesn't always succeed, he finds that he still grows through his failures and becomes more motivated as a result of them. Failures fuel his drive to succeed, to reach out to the right people for support or to learn a new skill to help him get there. He says his weakness is that he struggles to stay on track and focused, but that he mitigates this by surrounding himself with the right people who give him honest and loving feedback.

I asked Adam for his tips based on what he's learnt about success and setting goals. He gave me this list:

- *Be honest with yourself. We all have doubts, and we all struggle to make choices in life, but when you dig deep and are honest with yourself you'll always feel better about the choices you make.*

- *Always surround yourself with people who are not afraid to have the hard conversations with you. Those are the people who will continue to add value to everything you do.*

- *Own everything you do. The good, the bad and the ugly.*

On owning your choices, Adam says, 'Ownership is the one trait that's been the most valuable to me. With ownership you have control over how you accept and move forward with the things you do, this has what has helped me work through the many challenges I have faced in life and helped me not be a victim.'

I chose Adam's story to conclude this book because it wraps up so many of the themes I've mentioned. Firstly, I respect his mental conditioning. His mindset is fit enough to accept the circumstances he finds himself in and behave in a way that moves him forward. He also shows perseverance. Despite all the odds, Adam perseveres with his pursuit of making a meaningful contribution to the world. He puts in the maximum effort he can to succeed, even when he faces significant challenges! And you can see the result of his mindset has been personal growth and development.

In fact, in every story I mentioned throughout this book you will see how each person has perfectly articulated what I hope this book will provide you with. Their journeys summarised the mindset required to succeed without burning out and dipped into the themes such as:

1. *Setting meaningful goals*

2. *Increasing willpower, discipline and motivation with good habits*

3. *Preventing burnout by not mindlessly pursuing goals that aren't meaningful*

4. *Choosing new goals outside of comfort zones*

5. *Being flexible in your thinking by learning from success and failures, maintaining perspective and practising gratitude*

6. *Maintaining strength by chunking down goals into smaller parts, recruiting support, and managing worry*

7. *Building endurance and resilience by aligning goals to long-term vision and values, labelling emotions, and seeing new opportunities*

8. *Guarding the composition of thoughts by being realistically optimistic, decluttering and focusing, and protecting against naysayers*

I hope that the stories in this book have shown you that ordinary people do extraordinary things, purely by practising the right mindset.

I hope their journeys have inspired you as much as they've inspired me. Remember, that a few small workouts per day build up to have a considerable impact. And soon enough, you too will be running those mental marathons, and without breaking a sweat.

Good luck!

Luisa Hogan

vermelho

We pride ourselves in bringing the adaptable, swift and fun energy of the hummingbird to you.

We offer a full suite of services that can be blended and tailored just for you. We support businesses, corporate teams, community organisations and schools to have happier, resilient teams with the right mindset to lead change. We also work one-on-one with individuals looking to boost their development, reach their goals, and improve their mindset.

Consulting Services | Tailored Workshops and Facilitation | Coaching | Key Notes and Conferences

www.vermelho.com.au

info@vermelho.com.au